RACE AND ETHNICITY

THE BASICS

Peter Kivisto and Paul R. Croll

Routledge
Taylor & Francis Group

LONDON AND NEW YORK

First published 2012
by Routledge
2 Park Square, Milton Park, Abingdon, Oxon OX14 4RN

Simultaneously published in the USA and Canada
by Routledge
711 Third Avenue, New York, NY 10017

*Routledge is an imprint of the Taylor & Francis Group, an informa
business*

British Library Cataloguing in Publication Data
A catalogue record for this book is available from the British Library

Library of Congress Cataloging in Publication Data
Kivisto, Peter, 1948-
Race and ethnicity : the basics / Peter Kivisto and Paul Croll.
p. cm. – (The basics)
Includes bibliographical references.
1. Race. 2. Racism. 3. Ethnicity. 4. Ethnic groups. I. Croll, Paul. II. Title.
HT1521.K49 2012
305.8–dc23
2011020296

ISBN: 978-0-415-77373-7 (hbk)
ISBN: 978-0-415-77374-4 (pbk)
ISBN: 978-0-203-18107-2 (ebk)

Typeset in Aldus and Scala Sans
by Saxon Graphics Ltd, Derby

MIX
Paper from
responsible sources
FSC   FSC® C004839
www.fsc.org

Printed and bound in Great Britain by
TJ International Ltd, Padstow, Cornwall

CONTENTS

LIST OF ILLUSTRATIONS

FIGURES

TABLES

BOXES

ACKNOWLEDGEMENTS

Figure 1.2 Reproduced by permission of the American Anthropological Association from its RACE: Are We So Different? public education project. Not for sale or further reproduction

Figure 2.3 Data from The Gallup Minority Rights and Relations Survey 2007

Figure 3.1 Data from US Census Bureau, Current Population Survey. 1968 to 2010 Annual Social and Economic Supplements

Figure 3.2 Data from US Census Bureau of Labor Statistics

Figure 3.3 Data from Center for American Progress

Figure 3.4 Data from Federal Reserve, 2007 Survey of Consumer Finances Public Data Set

Figure 3.5 Data from Corporation for Enterprise Development, 2007-2008 Assets and Opportunity Scorecard

Figure 3.6 Data from US Census Current Population Survey 2005

Figure 4.1 Sabrina Coffey

Figure 4.2 US Holocaust Memorial Museum

Figure 5.1 Sabrina Coffey

AUTHOR ACKNOWLEDGEMENTS

We would like to single out for special thanks our departmental secretary Jean Sottos and two of our students who took a lead role in producing various boxes and figures for the book: Sabrina Coffey and Moselle Singh. In addition, we would like to thank our departmental colleagues for their support and, more importantly, for their good will. Finally, we want our families to know that we truly appreciate their encouragement throughout. We understand only too well that our preoccupation with the book took away from precious time with each and every one of you.

DEFINING THE SUBJECT

Race and **ethnicity** have, during the centuries since the advent of the modern nation-state and the era of colonialism, profoundly shaped the social, cultural, economic, and political character of much of the globe. This includes both the wealthy nations of the world and the poor ones. Contrary to the predictions of modernization theorists and Marxists, both of which foresaw a future in which race and ethnicity would decline in significance as a consequence of the evolution of capitalist industrialization or the more overarching impact of the totality of modern institutions and practices, the historical record clearly reveals that divisions based on race and ethnicity remain a salient feature of contemporary social life in the twenty-first century.

Indeed, to categorize people in everyday conversations along the lines of racial or ethnic group affiliations is commonplace. Thus, in the US to speak of African Americans or blacks is to lump approximately 12 percent of the nation's population into one of the five prominently identified races in the nation. On the other hand, to speak about Swedish Americans or Italian Americans—equally commonplace—is to place millions of people into what are seen as the vast array of ethnic groups residing in the nation. A similar pattern can be seen in the UK, where the term "black" was used a few decades ago to describe the post-World War II immigrants coming largely from the Caribbean and the Indian subcontinent, in this case the term black being used more broadly than in the US context. Over time, these two groups would be distinguished, respectively as Afro-Caribbeans and Asians. At the same time, the UK used the term ethnic or national group to refer to Scots and the Welsh, two groups with historic roots in the nation as deep as are those of the English.

In these examples of the way these two terms are used, there appears to be a distinction being made wherein race refers to biological or physiological differences, while ethnic refers to cultural differences. In practice, however, the two are often more interconnected, convoluted, and subject to historical change. Thus, Jews throughout Western Europe and North America were viewed in both racial and ethnic terms during the nineteenth century and the early part of the twentieth. However, after the Holocaust, a pronounced shift occurred in all of these nations that resulted in locating Jews racially in the same racial grouping as the majority population, which meant that they were considered to be white. At the same time, they were defined as being a distinctive ethnic group within that racial category.

To complicate matters further, in some societies people are placed into categories in an either/or fashion. One is either white or black. Nowhere was this more evident than in the US for much of its history, where what became known as the "one-drop" rule prevailed. What this rule meant was that any person with the slightest amount of black ancestry would be considered black. In one illustration of this phenomenon, a woman in Louisiana who was 1/32 black and thus 31/32s white sought to have her race listed as white on her driver's license. The state denied that request and prevailed in the courts. The consequence of this approach is that a public recognition of race mixing is repressed. It should be noted that the mixed race individual is defined as being a member of the subordinate group, not the dominant group. This is a mode of categorizing people based on what is termed "**hypodescent**."

Of course, race and ethnicity would not be such controversial topics if all that was involved was categorization. But the history of the use of these terms reveals that to categorize is to place people in a hierarchy that defines groups in terms of whether they are to be favored or not, privileged or not, empowered or not, economically advantaged or not, and so forth. Moreover, history also reveals that dividing people along racial and ethnic lines has generated forms of intra-group conflict, coercion, and violence, including in the most extreme forms of conflict attempts to exterminate an entire group. The genocidal campaigns that the world has witnessed during the past century, from the Armenian **genocide** after World War I to the ghastly attempt by the Nazi regime to destroy European Jewry, through to the campaign of extermination that Hutus undertook against the Tutsis in Rwanda and the **ethnic cleansing** in Bosnia that sought to kill off the territory's Muslim community reveal the continual threat of barbarism in the modern world.

If this was the whole story, it would clearly be best to do whatever can be done to eliminate or reduce as much as possible ethnic and racial definitions. However, these forms of identity have not simply been a source of conflict, but have often been a more positive source of personal identity and group affiliation, offering people a way to create a meaningful life. A shared history and culture can provide people with a source of strength that can help them meet various challenges collectively.

Given the Janus face of race and ethnicity and their continuing importance, the challenge is to better understand them in order to promote that which is positive while combating the negative. Sociology and anthropology, the closest of social science relatives, have from their respective origins paid considerable attention to race and ethnicity, and thus contemporary scholars build on a long and productive tradition of empirical research and theoretical development. Indeed, the sheer volume of published works in this field can quickly overwhelm the student novice. This book is conceived with this fact in mind. Its purpose, quite simply, is to acquaint students and other interested readers with the sociological subfield devoted to the social scientific understanding of the forms and dynamics of racial and ethnic relations. In this regard, one caveat at the outset is in order. While the issues discussed below are applicable in any and all national contexts, our examples will chiefly be drawn from major English-speaking industrial nations, which will be the places that most of our readers will be most familiar with.

Before turning to four substantive topics addressing respectively **prejudice** and **discrimination**, the dynamics of inequality, ethnic conflict, and modes of incorporation of ethnic and racial groups, we spend time in this chapter clarifying what exactly the subject matter at hand is, beginning with a look at the nature of the relationship between race and ethnicity.

HOW ARE RACE AND ETHNICITY RELATED?

There is at the moment a discussion about whether it's a mistake to talk about racial or ethnic *groups* (Brubaker 2004). The rub, according to those who have called this common practice into question is that two things tend to happen when we discuss ethnicity or race in terms of groups: groups are essentialized and they are viewed as homogeneous. To say they are essentialized means that groups are seen as fixed and determinate, and not subject to change over time. The concern about homogeneity points to the fact that to speak about a group can imply that it can be seen as referring to all members of the group without regard to internal differences. We understand the concerns of those who have advocated for a way of viewing ethnicity and race that takes us "beyond groupism" (Brubaker 2004: 11), but think that it is not only unlikely that people will abandon referring to groups, but unnecessary to do so since properly understood, such language is a convenient shorthand.

The question to be addressed in this section concerns the relationship between racial groups and ethnic groups. As Figure 1.1 illustrates, we will examine three different answers to the question. The first suggests that racial groups and ethnic groups are two different types of group. The second position claims that while racial and ethnic groups are usually distinct, in some circumstances they are overlapping. The third views racial groups as a subset of ethnic groups.

An immediate issue arises in any effort to decide which of these three perspectives is more persuasive. Are we interested in determining how ordinary people understand the relationship, or are we trying to make an assessment based on an analytical perspective useful for sociological inquiry? While both are reasonable ways of answering the question, we are concerned here with these terms as sociological concepts. That being said, it is often difficult for sociologists to neatly separate everyday usage from sociological concepts, due to the fact that the latter is derivative of and embedded in the former.

RACE AND THE COLONIAL LEGACY

Race was used far earlier than ethnicity in everyday discourse. The beginning of modern notions of race coincided with the European colonization of the world, at which time contact, conflict, and the

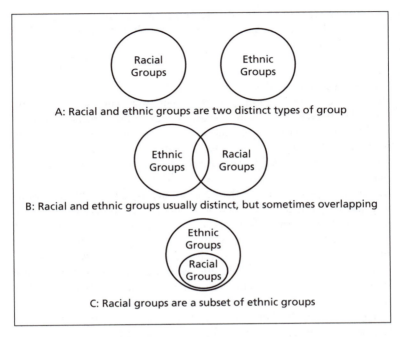

A: Racial and ethnic groups are two distinct types of group

B: Racial and ethnic groups usually distinct, but sometimes overlapping

C: Racial groups are a subset of ethnic groups

Figure 1.1: The relationship of racial groups to ethnic groups: competing conceptual models.

oppression of people from the "New World" with different physical features and different cultures led to an ongoing debate about the human character of the "other." European commentators, using their own civilization as a standard by which other civilizations would be judged, tended to find them wanting. Their ethnocentric perspective on the world sometimes led them to conclude that the "other" was not fully human. At other times, they distinguished their "civilized" world from that of the "barbarians." It was the rare humanist who could see through this viewpoint. However, a minority opinion shared the enlightened perspective of the great sixteenth-century French essayist Michel de Montaigne, who in his essay "Of Cannibals" (written in response to seeing a cannibal brought to France by an explorer) wrote,

> I think there is nothing barbarous and savage in that nation, from what I have been told, except that each man calls barbarism whatever is not

his own practice; for indeed it seems we have no other test of truth and
reason than the example and pattern of the opinions and customs of the
country we live in

(Montaigne 1958: 152)

The **ethnocentrism** that Montaigne tried to challenge succeeded in
shaping our understanding of race. The Swedish naturalist Carl
Linnaeus offered the first of numerous "scientific" efforts to classify
the human population by breaking it into various races. Specifically,
he divided humankind into four major racial groups: white, red,
yellow and black. While this might at some level be seen as a
reasonable broad generalization about differences in skin coloration,
he meant it to be far more than a mere description of differences in
physical appearance. In his view, the physical differences were deeply
interconnected with differences in temperament, intelligence, and
moral worthiness. Linnaeus assumed that racial differences could
speak to determining who was capable of reason and who was not,
who was morally responsible and who was not, who was fit for
leadership and who was destined to be led, and who was understandably
the conqueror and who was the conquered.

This sort of thinking characterized the nineteenth and early
twentieth centuries, as witnessed in Comte Arthur de Gobineau's *The
Inequality of Human Races* (1915[1853–1855]). Gobineau's work set
the tone for a century of writing on race, where the goal was not only
to classify people along racial lines, but to highlight the presumed
superiority of some groups and the inferiority of others. He was
especially interested in differentiating strong and weak groups,
contending that because the strong exhibited a willingness to migrate,
they would inevitably conquer the weak, and in the process bring to
them the benefits of civilization. Billed as science, what Gobineau
actually produced was an ideological defense of European colonialism.

Such thinking permeated **Social Darwinian** ideology, with its
belief in societal evolution and emphasis on the survival of the fittest.
It offered a critique of those seeking to launch some form of a welfare
state, wherein all of the members of a society would be accorded as
fundamental rights a certain bedrock standard of living. According to
Social Darwinists, to do so would amount to undermining the overall
health of the society by preventing its weak and unhealthy elements
from being eliminated naturally. This political worldview painted a

picture of incessant struggle and conflict, a world that was "red in tooth and claw." Such a perspective could lead to the promotion of such draconian positions as the suggestion supported by Franklin Giddings, prominent American sociologist and officer in the Immigration Restriction League, to force poor immigrants into workhouses where they would be prevented from producing any more children. It also fit in well with the **Eugenics** movement, first advocated by Sir Francis Galton (half-cousin to Charles Darwin), that sought to employ genetics to improve the human race through selective breeding.

Racialist thinking divided the peoples occupying the European continent further into subsets of the white race, with a division between the Teutonic, Alpine, and Mediterranean that was developed by William Z. Ripley (1899) being one such prominent example. The purpose of making such distinctions was not simply to determine difference, but to rank those differences on a racial hierarchy. Ripley and his peers always placed the Teutonic race on the top of the hierarchy and the Mediterranean race on the bottom. Considerable energy was devoted to attempting to place various groups into these categories. In this task, some groups proved to be especially problematic, such as Jews and Lapps. The former seemed not to fit into any of the three races, while the latter was suspected of having ancient origins in Asia.

As historian Nell Irvin Painter (2010) has stressed, these and similar efforts aimed at creating classificatory schemes of racial categorization were never done in a disinterested attempt to depict human diversity. Rather, the project was always designed to advance the argument on behalf of the existence of racial hierarchies as permanent, biologically rooted features of human diversity. As such, the project's purpose was to determine standards for adjudicating racial superiority and inferiority along the lines of intelligence and moral character. As such, racialist thinking served as a powerful ideological tool justifying oppression and exploitation. It provided a rationalization for European colonialism, for slavery, and for the subjugation of **indigenous peoples** by the charter members of settler nations such as Australia, Canada, and the US.

WHEN DID ETHNICITY COME INTO VOGUE?

Werner Sollors (1986) has pointed out that the word ethnicity didn't come into common usage until the 1930s, which coincides with the rise of Nazi Germany, whose official ideologues embraced the sort of racialist thought we've been describing. As a way of distancing themselves from the racism inherent in racialist thinking, some scholars tried to implement an alternative language. Michael Banton (1987: xi) points to the case of two prominent anthropologists, Sir Julian Huxley and A. C. Haddon, who "criticized mistaken racial doctrines and proposed the use of 'ethnic group' in place of 'race' when discussing the social aspect, because the adjective 'ethnic' more clearly indicated a concern with social differences."

Note what they were proposing. They did not necessarily want to discard the term "race," but instead wanted to limit its use to the non-social, which one can assume meant the biological. Huxley and Haddon were not alone in turning to ethnicity. The prominent figures associated with the Chicago School of Sociology, especially W. I. Thomas and Robert E. Park, increasingly sought to distance themselves from biologically rooted explanations by employing accounts rooted in culture and social structure. By the publication of the landmark Yankee City studies in the 1940s, led by Chicago sociologist W. Lloyd Warner (1963), it was clear that ethnicity was in vogue. However, the more social scientists used the term, the more it entered everyday language. A few years after World War II ended, Everett C. Hughes (1971[1948]: 153) described the term "ethnic group" as a "colorless catch-all much used by anthropologists and sociologists," going on to predict that as it was increasingly "taken up by a larger public," scholars would have to seek yet another serviceable term.

RACE AND ETHNICITY

Six decades later, we haven't followed Hughes' advice, but instead continue to debate the merits of race versus ethnicity and seek to sort out their relationship. With this brief historical excursus on origins of these two terms completed, we turn below to an assessment of the merits of each of the three competing positions.

RACE AND ETHNICITY AS DISTINCT

Perhaps the most influential scholars to make the case for distinguishing racial groups from ethnic groups are Michael Omi and Howard Winant, in *Racial Formation in the United States* (1994). In their view, ethnic groups should be used to refer to those groups of voluntary immigrants who left their homelands in various points in Europe for the US, while race is especially apt in discussing African Americans and Native Americans. The rationale for making this distinction is that these groups have had very different historical experiences. While voluntary immigrants from Europe often confronted prejudice and discrimination, they experienced nothing resembling the oppression and marginalization that involuntary migrants who were forced into slavery experienced or that the victims of colonial domination were forced to endure. Distinguishing between ethnic and racial groups is meant to serve as a reminder of the vastly different histories of voluntary immigrants versus others. Omi and Winant appear to want to locate Latinos and Asians in the race category, though in many respects their histories more closely resemble their immigrant counterparts from Europe. It is true that they did confront far more intense nativist hostility and have had a considerably more difficult time finding a foothold in their new homeland than was the case with European-origin groups, but they were for the most part voluntary labor migrants (the history of Mexicans in the US is complicated, and thus the qualifier).

Although Omi and Winant operate from a social constructionist perspective, their work appeared before the arrival of "whiteness studies," which sought to indicate that many European immigrant groups were not, upon arrival, seen as white. Rather, through a process of political and social claims-making, many of these groups engaged in a long process of, to use the words of the preeminent whiteness studies historian David Roediger (2005), "working toward whiteness." Omi and Winant's lack of attention to the racialized language used to depict many—though not all—European immigrant groups when they first arrived in America led them to make a distinction that the historical evidence is hard to sustain.

An additional problem with Omi and Winant's argument is that despite their social constructionist perspective, there is a tendency to **essentialize** race. Unlike the presumed fluidity of ethnic identities, race seems at their hands to take on a much more unchanging character. The underlying problem we have with their argument is that it confuses a historical distinction with an analytical one. It conflates analytical categories with everyday applied uses of both terms. It is for this reason that we don't find this dichotomous position to be very convincing.

RACE AND ETHNICITY AS OVERLAPPING

An intermediate position can be found in the work of Stephen Cornell and Douglas Hartmann in their widely-cited *Ethnicity and Race: Making Identities in a Changing World* (2007). In their view, race and ethnicity should be viewed as different though not always mutually exclusive. Their argument can be summarized as follows:

- Similar to Omi and Winant, Cornell and Hartmann contend that groups defined as racial have usually had considerably different historical experiences from groups defined as ethnic.
- Race has proven in most instances to be the most powerful dividing line in societies, establishing boundaries between us and them. If an individual can be identified with both an ethnic and racial label, the latter will likely be more consequential in defining boundaries (thus, that a person is identified as an Asian American will be more significant in determining life chances than being defined as Chinese American).
- Race became the major mode of group differentiation as a result of the meeting of peoples on the global racial frontiers during the era of European colonial expansion.
- Race more than ethnicity is defined in terms of power relations, with racial ideologies serving as a rationale for particular groups to achieve domination over other groups.
- Related to the above, racial categories are conceived in terms of differences in the worth and abilities of groups. Simply put, racial designations are conceived in terms of creating group hierarchies predicated on assessments of superiority and inferiority.
- Race in contrast to ethnicity is more often viewed as a natural category, which means that it is permanent, whereas ethnicity is subject to historical modification.
- Race tends to be imputed to groups by powerful outside groups, while ethnicity is often claimed by the groups themselves.

(Cornell and Hartmann 2007: 26–32)

Despite these differences, Cornell and Hartmann contend that there are empirical instances in which race and ethnicity overlap and cannot be distinguished as neatly as Omi and Winant sought to do. They offer a number of examples that challenge the differences noted above. Thus, in Belgium, the major societal dividing line is between the Flemish and Walloon ethnic communities, rather than being predicated on race. They can point to cases where ethnicity is assigned by others, with the members of the group having little say in the matter. In short, instead of the sharp distinction of the previous account, this one blurs the boundaries.

That being said, the chief problem noted for the first model applies here as well. Once again, the problem is that Cornell and Hartmann conflate historical and analytical approaches to the subject, shaping the latter by the former.

RACE AS A SUBSET OF ETHNICITY

In providing an alternative to these two approaches, treating race as a subset of ethnicity is an effort to offer an analytical model that can be distinguished from historical or everyday uses. It does so by treating ethnicity as a concept with a fairly explicit definition. What did sociologists and anthropologists have in mind when they began to use this "colorless catch-all" term? In the first place, it referred to groups that shared a common history—real or perceived—and with it a sense of a common geographic origin. It also refers to a shared culture, which is a broad term that can include within it traditions, folkways, values, symbols, language, and religion. Moreover, given that ethnicity is a boundary creating construct, it refers to a belief among group members and outsiders alike that it constitutes a distinctive community formation. Finally, and this is key, race can be seen as one other potential component of ethnic identity and group definition.

To the extent that in any particular instance race is highly salient, it is appropriate to speak of a *racialized ethnicity*. In this regard, race would be similar to religion, as we shall see in the next section. In some instances, religion is a particularly significant aspect of an ethnic identity, while in other instances it is not. For Jews in the US, religion is a crucially vital aspect of ethnic identity, while for Germans it is less so. Such is also the case with race. Clearly US history has been profoundly shaped by the unequal and inequitable relationship between Americans of African descent and those of European origin. A parallel situation does not exist in Canada, where the major divide between the nation's two "charter groups," British Canadians and French Canadians is not predicated on the understanding that their differences are based on race.

A key virtue of treating race as a subset of ethnicity is that it prevents viewing the former in terms of nature and the latter in terms of culture. Historian Linda Nicholson (2008: 11–20) has observed that during the nineteenth century, when racialist thinking took on a "scientific" cast, the emphasis was on the naturalness of race, which meant that racial groups were posited to exist in a fixed and unchanging racial hierarchy. While advocates for the first two positions discussed above seek to avoid such naturalizing tendencies in their effort to treat race and ethnicity from a social constructionist perspective, it is our sense that maintaining the distinction they seek to does not serve that purpose well.

Instead, by speaking of racialized ethnicity, it is clear that what is at stake entails coming to terms with socially created and embedded notions about group differences predicated on observable physiological differences that are defined as having consequences for innate ability, moral character, and persistent inequality. In short, from this perspective race can be seen for what it is: a definition of the situation that, to the extent that it is embraced by large numbers of people, will have real consequences in the social world.

British cultural sociologist Paul Gilroy (2000: 1) has challenged those who want to maintain a distinction between race and ethnicity, arguing that it is preferable to consider

> patterns of conflict connected to the consolidation of *cultural lines* rather than color lines and is concerned, in particular, with the operations of power, which, thanks to ideas about "race", have become entangled with those vain and mistaken attempts to delineate and subdivide humankind.

In even more explicit terms, Harvard sociologist Orlando Patterson (1997: 173) contends that, "The term *race* itself should be abandoned … and the distinction between 'race' and ethnicity should be abandoned as meaningless and potentially dangerous."

The suggestion advanced herein is not to abandon the term race, but to understand it in context. Ethnicity, quite simply, is the umbrella term that encompasses race, religion, language, and other factors that can, depending on the particular case, play a greater or lesser role. In this regard, we concur with Sandra Wallman (1986: 230) that race is but one element to be used as an ethnic boundary marker, others including language, religion, shared history, shared traditions, and a common geographic origin; and with Susan Olzak (1992: 25, emphasis in the original) when she contends that "*race* is a specific instance of ethnicity, defined by membership based on what are *assumed to be* inherited phenotypical characteristics." Similarly, Floya Anathias

(1992: 421) is correct in claiming that " 'race' categories belong to the more encompassing category of ethnic collectivity." Moreover, as Steve Fenton (1999: 4) has observed in a passage that succinctly summarizes our position, "The term 'ethnic' has a much greater claim to analytical usefulness in sociology because it is not hampered by a history of connotations with discredited science and malevolent practices in the way the term 'race' is." One of the implications of this position is that when race does prove to be an especially important aspect of ethnic identity, the focus will be less on race per se than on racism and its consequences. This is what Robert Miles and Malcolm Brown (2003) had in mind in arguing for refocusing research from an emphasis on "race relations" to racism.

All this being said, it is difficult to break from using the altogether commonplace "race and ethnicity" couplet. In what follows we will continue to write about race and ethnicity, but only because it is a familiar shorthand, easier than writing over and over again "ethnicity, including racialized ethnicity." Moreover, both race and ethnicity are categories of practice, which means that we need to consider how they are defined and used both in the everyday discourse of ordinary people—both members of the dominant society and members of minority groups—and in the creation of official government classificatory schemes (Brubaker 2004: 31).

RACE AND ETHNICITY AS SOCIAL CONSTRUCTIONS

Race and ethnicity are social constructions. This phrase is often used by academics when discussing the nature of race and ethnicity. But what does it mean? What is the significance of this notion? One of the most important aspects of this idea is that both race and ethnicity are dependent upon the particular social and historical contexts in which they occur. We observe race and ethnicity all around us, in our daily lives, at school, at work, in the media. With race and ethnicity all around us, it is easy to assume that they are natural, inherent categories that have always existed and will always exist, virtually unchanged. As noted earlier, we refer to the tendency to view race and ethnicity in this way as "essentializing" them.

When people do so, they assume that the racial and ethnic categories they use and understand are the same across societies and over time. However, anyone who has examined the history of the ways each term has been used will quickly be disabused of such a belief. Historians and social scientists have offered us clear evidence that these two concepts, indeed, have changed over time, acquiring different meanings and leading to widely varied consequences.

HISTORICAL CHANGE

Figure 1.2 is a photo that came from an exhibit entitled "Race: Are We So Different?" that traveled around science museums across the US a few years ago. On each person's shirt are the various labels that the US Census Bureau has used at various times since the first census in 1790 up to and including the 2000 census (the exhibit took place prior to the 2010 census). A cursory examination of the photo reveals that the categories have not remained constant. Thus, the prefix "free" that described the person in the left of the back row in the first census was subsequently dropped, the assumption being that if one was white, one was free. Sometimes the words change but the category

Figure 1.2: Changing census terminology.

remains the same: thus, as the Civil War began, a person was black, while immediately after World War II that person was a Negro. Four decades later, and the person was again black. As this example indicates, these categories reflect, at least in part, changes in public opinion, which at various junctures the government needs to take seriously.

The person in the far right of the back row reveals yet another way that categories change. In the first census of the twentieth century, this individual would have been classified as Japanese, referring to a specific nationality or ethnic group. However, by the last census of that century, the category had become **panethnic** with the use of the term "Asian." Finally, while the person second from the left in the back row was in the past defined solely in terms of a presumably racial category, in 1980 that person was listed as Hispanic black—a term that seeks to combine what the Census Bureau viewed as an ethnic and a racial category.

In short, this photo offers plenty of evidence that racial and ethnic categories are not immutable givens. Rather, they have been socially constructed. In this example, the government played the dominant role in the process, with a behind the scenes role played by the public at large. However, this isn't the whole story. If ethnic and racial groups are created, the people who become members of these collectivities also play a role in their development—sometimes a dominant role, sometimes not.

Another example that derives from an approach to this field known as whiteness studies, a topic we will discuss in the next chapter, can be observed by examining the complex story of immigration to the US for certain white ethnic groups, beginning with the Irish. Many European immigrants were not considered to be white when they first arrived in America, and what ensued was a struggle to "become white." While it is true that in the twenty-first century, Irish Americans are considered without question to be white, when Irish immigrants arrived in the early nineteenth century, they were subject to many of the same stereotypes, prejudices, and discrimination imposed upon disadvantaged, non-European origin groups. There were fears of Irish immigrants marrying native-born whites and established groups in society at the time questioned their morals and values (Ignatiev 1995).

THE ROLE OF PLACE

In addition to variations across time, a comparison of racial and ethnic categories across societies shows that race and ethnicity also vary by place. Some nations, such as Brazil and a number of Caribbean countries, do not operate with a view of race that is constructed in binary terms, such that a person is either white or black. Instead, these nations recognize the reality of racial mixing and thus have constructed categories to account for this reality. Thus, the term "**mulatto**," which refers to a person of mixed white/European and black/African parentage is a commonly used term (in Brazil "pardo" is used as a synonym for mulatto). Less commonly used, but used nonetheless, are the terms "quadroon" and octoroon," referring respectively to individuals who are one-fourth black and one-eighth black. Meanwhile, the term "**mestizo**" describes an individual who is the product of white/European and indigenous/Indian ancestry.

South Africa during the era of apartheid constructed a racial system consisting of four groups: whites (which consisted chiefly of Boers, or people of Dutch ancestry, and the British), blacks, coloreds (the term used for people of mixed black and white ancestry), and Indian, a category that reflected the significance of immigrants from India in South Africa's history. These examples stand in contrast to the hypodescent system in the US that was described earlier in the chapter.

One further comparative illustration serves to reveal just how nationally specific official categorizations of race actually are. At the beginning of the current century, the United States government specified five broad racial groups: White, American Indian (plus Alaskan Natives), Blacks (or African Americans), Asians (including Native Hawaiians or Other Pacific Islanders), and Some Other Race. Note that Hispanic or Latino was not defined as one of the racial categories. Rather, it was defined as an ethnic identity. In terms of ethnicity, people were asked if they were Hispanic/Latino or non-Hispanic/non-Latino. Thus all respondents were asked two questions, one that located themselves ethnically and the other racially. During the same timeframe, the Office for National Statistics in the United Kingdom specified the following racial categories in England and Wales (they used a somewhat different set of categories for Scotland and Northern Ireland): White, Mixed, Asian or Asian British, Black or Black British, and Chinese or Other Ethnic Group. Note, for example, how differently the term Asian is used in the two national contexts. Meanwhile, in France the government has refused to collect census data on racial groups, in fact making such an effort illegal. Thus, at the moment as an official governmental category of practice, there are no ethnic or racial groups in France (recently, the government of Nicolas Sarkozy has created a commission to see if this policy ought to be reconsidered).

FUTURE PROSPECTS

Given these variations across time and place, it is reasonable to expect that the content of racial and ethnic categories will continue to change in order to address novel circumstances. Looking at the US, there is currently a widely-held notion circulating among the public that the country will become "majority non-white" by 2050. But it is important here to note that this assumption is based on present understandings of racial and ethnic categories and on population projections of current trends. How will racial and ethnic categories be defined when the US is no longer a "majority white" society? An even better question to ask may be what "white" will look like in 2050? Who will be part of the "white" racial group? Who will not? Asking these questions help us to remember the social construction of these categories.

Herbert Gans (1999) has suggested that whereas in the past, the broadest division in the nation was between whites and nonwhites, which largely came down to a division between European-origin peoples and everyone else, what might be happening at the beginning of the current century, he speculated, was a new divide: between blacks and non-blacks. What this would mean is that those of European-origin would be joined in one large bloc by Asians, Latinos, and Native Americans, leaving the 14 percent of the population that is black in a category by itself.

SOCIAL CONSTRUCTION AND BIOLOGY

If racial and ethnic identities are social constructions, does this mean that biology is irrelevant? One particular place where this question has been posed concerns the current debates about genetics, DNA, and racial profiling. In recent years, scientific advances, including those associated with the Human Genome Project, have allowed genetic markers and information to enter both the courtroom and the doctor's office. Information from DNA samples at crime scenes is being used with increased frequency to attempt to identify the race or ethnicity of suspects. The medical community is using genetic information to identity racial and ethnic differences in susceptibility to various diseases and differences in responses to medications, which has led to the introduction of "designer drugs" targeted to specific racial and ethnic groups. For example, the drug BiDil is being specifically marketed as a prescription drug for African Americans with cardiovascular disease, it being the first drug to receive the approval of the Food and Drug Administration "exclusively for a racially identified population" (Lee 2005: 2136).

Troy Duster (2003, 2006) suggests that we need to place these scientific advances into historical context. In previous eras, other forms of the "science of race" were purported to offer biological accounts of racial differences regarding such things as intelligence and moral character. All have subsequently been debunked as empirically false. These include practices such as phrenology, which refers to the measurement of head shape, size, and other characteristics of the skull to study human behavior and innate intelligence. The Eugenics movement is another example of science used to justify racist practices, offering a presumed scientific justification for the control and the perpetual subordination of disadvantaged racial and ethnic minorities. Today there is a consensus that these earlier efforts to create a science of race turned out to be instances of pseudo-science.

However, while there is general consensus that the biological essentialism of race generated from phrenology and Eugenics was not correct, scholars and the public in general are far less certain about how to view the findings of contemporary genetic research. Will we look back at the end of the twenty-first century and agree that science finally "got race right?" Or, as Duster (2003: 10) ponders, is it possible that the use of genetics and DNA in forensics, racial profiling, and medicine constitutes the "specter of an early twenty-first century equivalent of phrenology?" At the moment, it is impossible to answer that question with a sufficient degree of certainty to eliminate the concerns raised by Duster. While it is clear that the research done to date by pharmocogenomics researchers has steered clear of the concerns of earlier generations for adjudicating presumed differences in intelligence and moral character predicated on race, and some fellow scientists have expressed reservations about the merits of race targeting treatments for various physical diseases.

At the same time, though a minority position today, there continue to be efforts aimed at using science to prove that various racial minorities in the Western nations are inferior to whites. In the US, such efforts have received the sponsorship of right-wing funding institutions such as the Bradley Foundation and the Pioneer Fund. Perhaps the most influential and controversial product of this funding was the 1994 book authored by Richard Herrnstein and Charles Murray, *The Bell Curve*. One of the conclusions that would have no doubt disturbed their counterparts from an earlier era was that although whites were considered to have discernable higher average levels of intelligence than blacks and Latinos, in fact Asians had higher levels of intelligence than whites. The bottom-line conclusions drawn by the authors was that intelligence was the best predictor of socioeconomic success and that given the fact that it was to large extent genetically determined, nothing could be done to change that fact. The inevitable policy conclusion was reminiscent of the Social Darwinians of a century earlier, for like Herbert Spencer in the UK and William Graham Sumner in the US, Herrnstein and Murray argue against the welfare state for its efforts to ensure the survival of the least fit.

Critics did more than challenge the political implications of the book, which among other things would call for the end of welfare benefits to the poor, the dismantling of affirmative action programs, and an array of other programs targeted to disadvantaged populations—both along racial and class lines. In addition, social scientific critics turned their sights on the science behind *The Bell Curve* and after careful analyses found it to be in a variety of ways bad science, perhaps even like the work of an earlier period, pseudo-science (Fischer, *et al.* 1996). Despite all of the efforts by Herrnstein and Murray's sponsors to claim that they had no hidden political agenda, but were simply letting the chips fall where they may, in fact it was clear that the rationale for sponsoring such work in the first place was to bring science into the service of a right-wing agenda aimed at destroying the welfare states that all of the world's liberal democracies had established in the second half of the twentieth century in order to seek to address the problems and inequities that result from the unacceptably high levels of social inequality that result from capitalist economies if not constrained by state intervention.

ETHNICITY AND NATIONALISM

What is **nationalism** and what is its relationship to ethnicity? In answer to the first question, nationalism can be defined quite simply as an ideology that defines a collectivity composed of people who are seen to be part of the same political community. The basis for the existence of a community can rely on language, religion, ethnicity, or what are seen to be shared civic values—or various combinations of these features. Not surprisingly, depending on the specific society and historical period in question, the answer to the second question will vary widely. There are places and times where ethnicity and nationalism seem to be fused together, in societies where there is a significant level of ethnic commonality (or at least perceived commonality) across the nation at the time. In these cases, ethnicity plays a role in forming and solidifying national identity. Nations that have until fairly recently been quite ethnically homogeneous include the Nordic countries, with Iceland, due to its small size and remoteness, being one of the purest examples. Far more typical, however, are situations where there is ethnic diversity within nations, leading to a decoupling of ethnicity and nationalism, or at least a minimizing of the significance of the connection. At the other end of the spectrum from a country such as Iceland are the historic settler nations, which include Australia, Canada, New Zealand, and the US. Of course, the level of diversity and the nature of the link between ethnic groups and national identity not only varies by place and time, but also by the perception and social location of the observer.

One way to begin to understand the relationship between ethnicity and nationalism is to look at the historical formations of nations and the role that ethnicity may or may not have played in these formations. In *The Ethnic Origins of Nations*, Anthony D. Smith (1986: x) argues that in the formation of modern nations, "the 'roots' of these nations are to be found, both in a general way and in many specific cases, in the model of ethnic community prevalent in much of the recorded history across the globe." Smith's argument is that the traditions, values, symbols, and other cultural material found collectively within groups of people provide some of the materials necessary for modern nations to develop. Smith then uses the term **"ethnie"** to refer to the ethnic communities and symbols that played a foundational role in the creation of modern nations.

From his perspective, the relationship between ethnicity and nationalism is historical, functional, and sequential. While Smith believes that ethnic communities played a role in forming nations in the past, this historical relationship between ethnicity and nationalism is not well suited to explain the relationship of ethnicity and nationalism in these same nations today.

A significant factor in trying to understand the relationship between ethnicity and nationalism is whether nationalist ideology is defined in civic or ethnic terms. A focus on this distinction can lead to a productive typology of nationalist ideologies, which highlights how and where ethnicity plays an important role in the nation. This typology of the different kinds of nationalist identity can be found in Milton Esman's *An Introduction to Ethnic Conflict* (2004: 41–42) in which he discusses three different variations of nationalist ideology, highlighting how and where ethnicity plays an important role:

- *Ethnonationalism*: The belief that any people that aspires to political self-determination and self-rule is a nation and as such is entitled to independent statehood.
- *Civic nationalism*: A territorial concept, defining the nation as all persons regardless of ethnic provenance who accept the duties and responsibilities of citizenship.
- *Syncretic nationalism*: In multinational states that include two or more nations, syncretic nationalism is an ideology that attempts to construct a new, inclusive national sentiment that will subordinate and eventually supplant the original national sentiments of its component peoples.

Each of these three variations, or ideal-types of nationalist ideology, has different implications for the relationship between ethnicity and nationalism. The concept of ideal-types is mentioned here because these three variations are more pure and distinct than we expect to find when actually mapping this typology onto existing modern nations. Many nations, the US and France being two examples, believe in the ideology of civic nationalism, where every person regardless of ethnicity can be a full citizen, and yet these nations often have long histories of political and social exclusion limiting which groups of people can take full advantage of the rights and responsibilities contained within citizenship. Among the nations that continue to maintain an ideology predicated on ethnic nationalism Japan stands out as an especially vivid example.

Ethnicity plays a clear and central role in ethnonationalism, where one particular group of people forms a nation state. In these cases, the ethnic identity and culture of this group often plays a significant role in the development of the state. In describing this type of nationalist ideology, Esman discusses the role and place of minority ethnic groups in these nations and explains that the nation "may tolerate minorities in its midst" (Esman 2004: 41). But how minority ethnic groups are actually treated in nations built on an ethnonationalist identity varies greatly. Within nations with a syncretic nationalist identity, ethnicity is clear and visible in that the challenge is to bring together multiple groups of people into one nation. Esman (2004: 43) provides the example of the UK as a multinational state composed of English, Welsh, Scottish, and Northern Irish peoples. In this example, the ethnic identities of the various peoples are clear while "political elites have attempted, and with some success, to cultivate an overarching British identity that would coexist with and gradually supersede the national sentiments of its component peoples." The level of success needs to be tempered by the realization that the Scottish National Party remains committed to leaving Britain and becoming an independent country, while the "Troubles" in Northern Ireland are a not-too-distant memory. Another example is Spain, where Basques and Catalans constitute two significant mobilized ethnonationalist communities, and here again the central Spanish state has only partially succeeded in convincing most Basques and Catalans that they can maintain their distinctive identities while simultaneously identifying as Spanish.

The relationship between ethnicity and nationalism is clearly complex, as well as always grounded in particular historical and social contexts. Nonetheless, typologies of nationalism such as these can help make sense of the varied roles of ethnicity within nations. Knowledge of the traditional groups of people that existed regionally prior to nation formation, the ideologies employed when nation formation occurred, the ethnic history of the nation, and the current state of ethnic groups within the nation can all provide clues as to the nature of the relationship between ethnicity and nationalism in any particular example. From a social constructionist perspective, societies should be viewed as changing over time and so even if we can successfully map out the connections between ethnicity and nationalism today, studying the past reminds us that there is always the possibility that these connections will be reformulated in the future.

ETHNICITY AND RELIGION

In some instances, religion is a relatively insignificant aspect of ethnic identity, while in other cases it is of central importance. A frequently used term to describe the latter is religio-ethnic group, which implies a tight connection between religious affiliation and ethnic identity. This is but one of several possible linkages. Based on various efforts to create a typology of possible linkages, we can distinguish four different types: ethnic fusion, ethnic religion, religious ethnicity, and ethnic autonomy (Kivisto 2007). These are summarized in Table 1.1.

In the first group, religion serves as the fundamental basis of ethnicity. Examples of groups characterized by ethnic fusion are Hasidic Jews, the Amish, and Hutterites. In maintaining the powerful link between religion and ethnicity, such groups typically pay a price insofar as they end up remaining rather small, insular groups that do not reach out to outsiders by seeking to make them insiders. In general, this type is representative of a rather small percentage of any society.

In contrast, ethnic religion and religious ethnicity are quite common. Examples of ethnic religion include the Greek Orthodox, Dutch Reformed, and Scottish Presbyterian communities. In these

Table 1.1: Types of connections between ethnicity and religion

Type	Characteristics	Example
Ethnic fusion	Religion major foundation of ethnic identity	Amish
Ethnic religion	Ethnicity serves to reinforce and define religious identity	Greek Orthodox
Religious ethnicity	Religion belief and practice colored by ethnic identity	Irish Catholics
Religion and ethnic disjuncture	Religion an inconsequential component of ethnic identity	Romany

cases, ethnicity has a long historical link to religion, though is not as meshed as with ethnic fusion. Rather, the key to this type is that ethnicity serves to reinforce and strengthen religious identity. The reverse is the case for the third type, religious ethnicity. Here religion serves as a particularly important aspect of defining ethnic identity. This can be seen in the cases of Irish, Italian, and Polish Catholics as well as Danish, Finnish, Norwegian, and Swedish Lutherans. The linkage in religious ethnicity is more historically contingent than in instances of ethnic religion, and therefore more subject to change. Thus, the linkage between Scandinavian ancestry and Lutheranism in America is rooted in history, but today's Lutheran churches are less Scandinavian than they once were, in part due to the inclusion of other groups, including blacks and Latinos, but more significantly due to the widespread phenomenon of intermarriage among European-origin groups.

The fourth type depicts a situation where the linkage between religion and ethnicity is weak, tenuous, or nonexistent. An example of an ethnic group that is defined without significant reference to religion is the Romany—more commonly known previously as Gypsies.

It is important to note that while this typology is helpful insofar as it can offer a comparative portrait of the differing linkages between ethnicity and religion, such portraits capture the situation at a particular moment in time. As the example of changes within Lutheranism suggests, the linkages are capable of change over time, especially for ethnic religion and religious ethnicity. To the extent that people engage in religious switching, the linkages between ethnicity and religion are subject to ongoing revision.

CONCLUSION

Before sociologists can study any topic, it is essential that the topic be adequately defined. This has been the objective of this chapter, which began with an extended discussion of a perennial debate among scholars in the field regarding the precise nature of the relationship between race and ethnicity. Three commonly used approaches were reviewed, with an argument advanced for viewing race as a subset of ethnicity and with the introduction of the idea of racialized ethnicity. From there, we discussed what it means to view race and ethnicity as socially constructed. This led to further definitional clarification in the two discussions that rounded out the chapter, one concerning the relationship between ethnicity and nationalism and the other addressing the relationship between ethnicity and religion. With this basic conceptual framework in place, we can proceed to explore the central issues in each of the following four chapters with a shared vocabulary.

2

PREJUDICE AND DISCRIMINATION

What barriers do members of outgroups confront in attempting to be treated as equals and possessing the same ability to access valued resources as members of the ingroup? What prevents such groups from being treated with respect and dignity? Why do some groups confront efforts aimed at marginalizing and excluding them? How does one account for manifestations of intergroup hostility? These and related questions have been a central aspect of race and ethnic studies since the beginning. Of particular interest for sociologists and psychologists are questions concerning the nature and the causes of prejudice and discrimination. Prejudice refers to negative attitudes directed at individuals of groups on account of their membership in those groups, while discrimination refers to actions that have a negative impact on the life circumstances and life chances of individuals or groups (for a similar definition, see Brown 1995). These two distinct but obviously intertwined concepts will be examined in the following pages.

At the outset, we should note a few features of the chapter. First, from the discussion of the classics to contemporary theoretical developments, the focus is on the US. We are aware of the fact that during the second half of the past century, scholars elsewhere, certainly the UK, have also developed similar lines of inquiry. However, we would like to focus on the US because readers will be afforded the opportunity to see how a long tradition of thought has developed over time and in response to changing historical circumstances. Second, the focus of the chapter is on race, or to be even more specific, on black/white relations. In part, this is a reflection of the fact that prejudice and discrimination directed against white, European-origin ethnics in the US has declined considerably in recent decades. It has not disappeared, particularly in the case of anti-Semitic prejudice, but first and foremost in the minds of the theorists who highlight this chapter has been a concern for the situation confronting African Americans, both prior to and in the aftermath of the civil rights movement. Finally, religious groups are often the victims of prejudice and discrimination, and much of what follows in this chapter can be extrapolated to the case of religious minorities. Nowhere is this more evident than in the case of Muslims in Europe today, who are the victims of Islamophobia.

THREE CLASSIC FRAMEWORKS

Both sociology and psychology have contributed to our understanding of prejudice and discrimination, and over time there has been a considerable amount of collaboration between the two disciplines in coming to terms with this topic. In this section, we will explore three classic accounts, accounts that in varied ways have had an enduring impact on subsequent work in the field. We will examine the work of one influential psychologist—Gordon W. Allport—and two sociologists—Robert K. Merton and Herbert Blumer.

THE SOCIAL PSYCHOLOGY OF PREJUDICE: ALLPORT

In 1954, Allport, a professor at Harvard, published what would prove to be a landmark study, *The Nature of Prejudice*. In this work, he set out to make sense of the types of prejudice that one could readily observe in America in the 1950s. He first tried to understand why people would develop preconceived judgments, or prejudgments, about others. From there, he examined the particular type of prejudgments that he labeled as prejudice and what could distinguish prejudgments, or misconceptions, from prejudices. He begins with the idea that people out of necessity generalize and categorize in attempting to make sense of their society, including generalizing and categorizing people on the basis of their group affiliations or identities.

PREJUDICE AS LEARNED BEHAVIOR

Generalizations are the product of learning, though in making such assessments people are often equipped with limited actual knowledge of the groups in question. Often people's generalizations amount to misconceptions. Allport did not think that this necessarily meant that a person harbored prejudicial attitudes or beliefs about outgroup members. Key for him was whether or not a person was prepared, on the basis of new, disconfirming evidence, to reject earlier "erroneous judgments in light of new evidence" (Allport 1954: 9). A person who does revise previously held negative evaluations is not prejudiced, while a person who refuses to do so, no matter how much evidence can be brought to bear to discount the initial generalization, is prejudiced.

Why are some people prepared to revise their misconceptions while others resist such revision? Why are some people able to avoid translating prejudgments into prejudice while others aren't? Allport answered these questions by offering a psychological account. In the first place, acquiring prejudicial views is in part learned behavior, and in this regard he devotes considerable space to the role of socialization, both in childhood and later in life. Writing during the 1950s, when there was considerable concern about the loss of individual autonomy due to the impact of mass society in the Cold War, he also focused on the pressures for social conformity.

THE PREJUDICED PERSONALITY

Allport, like others of his generation of psychologists, was influenced by psychoanalytic thought and sought to incorporate this perspective in an effort to describe what he called the "prejudiced personality." In this regard, his work paralleled that of others writing around the same time, such as John Dollard (1937), who used frustration-aggression theory to account for the racism he studied first hand in the American South, and Theodor Adorno and colleagues, (1950), whose authoritarian personality study sought to explain the type of character structure that led to support for Nazism. At the other end of the spectrum of personality types, Allport described the tolerant personality. In making his case, it was clear that the prejudiced personality should not simply be seen as the product of learned behavior, for underlying the learned aspect of prejudice is a deeper and far more disturbing psychological dynamic—one that if not strictly pathological, borders on pathology.

Box 2.1: The nature of prejudice: an illustration using two cases.

Gordon Allport wanted to make clear to his readers what prejudice was, and what it wasn't. He provided two cases from research at the time to highlight the essential qualities of prejudice, as he defined it. The first case is that of an anthropologist who was living with Native Americans on a reservation. The anthropologist would not allow his children to live with him on the reservation. When his children visited the reservation, he would not allow his children to play with the Native American children. When people heard of the anthropologist's actions, they accused him of displaying racial prejudice. However, the anthropologist explained that there were a high number of cases of tuberculosis on the reservation and that he was fearful his children could get infected and die, as he was aware had happened to some children on the reservation. Allport's reason for using this example is that the anthropologist's actions were not based in any dislike or negative feelings toward the Native Americans, and thus this is not an example of prejudice.

In contrast, his second case demonstrates what he believes is prejudice. Allport describes a social scientific experiment carried out by a Canadian researcher. The experiment involved mailing letters to hotels and resorts asking if rooms were available for specific dates. Two different letters were sent to hotels. They were identical in every respect except that one letter was from "Mr. Greenberg" and the other was from "Mr. Lockwood." Almost all of the hotels replied to Mr. Lockwood (95 percent) and almost as many offered accommodations on the dates requested (93 percent). However, only 52 percent of the hotels even replied to Mr. Greenberg and only 36 percent offered accommodations on the same dates. Allport argues that this is a clear case of prejudice, one in which the managers of the hotels and resorts were prejudiced against Mr. Greenberg because they assumed he was

Jewish. According to Allport, the decision to reply or offer accommodations was "obviously not made on the merits of the individual, but on 'Mr. Greenberg's' supposed membership in a group. He suffered discourtesy and exclusion solely because of his name, which aroused a prejudgment of his desirability in the eyes of the hotel managers."

(Source: Allport 1954: 4–5)

PREJUDICIAL ATTITUDES AND DISCRIMINATORY BEHAVIOR: MERTON

In 1949, around the same time that Allport was working on his theory of the psychological roots of prejudice, Columbia University's Robert K. Merton provided one of the first sociological treatments of the varied possible relationships between prejudice and discrimination. In "Discrimination and the American Creed" Merton's central argument was that attitudes (prejudice) and behaviors (discrimination), though often intertwined, can vary independently. Merton developed a typology to better understand the possible relationships between prejudice and discrimination. Within this typology, Merton considered those who are prejudiced and those who are not, as well as those who discriminate and those who do not. His typology can be understood as a 2×2 table, which is reflected in Table 2.1.

The article is framed in terms of what Merton refers to as the "American Creed," which entails the belief that all people, irrespective of their racial, ethnic, or religious backgrounds, are entitled to full equality, to equal justice, and freedom. The creed operates at three levels: as an ideal, as an individual belief, and in individual conduct.

Table 2.1: Merton's typology

	Unprejudiced	*Prejudiced*
Non-Discriminator	All-Weather Liberal	Fair Weather Illiberal
Discriminator	Fair Weather Liberal	All Weather Illiberal

Merton was quite aware of the fact that during this period, shortly before the beginning of the civil rights movement, a majority of white Americans did not actually believe that blacks should be afforded equal opportunities in the acquisition of jobs or in the neighborhoods they lived in. His interest was in exploring the various ways that people could in beliefs and actions respond to the high principles articulated in the Declaration of Independence and the Constitution.

THE ALL-WEATHER LIBERAL

Merton considered four types. The first is what he refers to as the unprejudiced non-discriminator, or the All-Weather Liberal. This category describes individuals who embrace the ideals of the American creed, do not harbor prejudicial attitudes towards minority groups, and do not discriminate. Such individuals exhibit a consistency between their beliefs and their actions. Some within this group might be civil rights activists, translating their beliefs into actions designed to bring reality into consonance with the ideals of the creed. However, many may simply act out their beliefs in private, non-political ways.

THE ALL-WEATHER ILLIBERAL

At the other end of the spectrum is the prejudiced discriminator, or the All-Weather Illiberal. Merton (1949: 109) describes this person aptly as "the bigot pure and unashamed, the man of prejudice consistent in his departure from the American creed." Such a person rejects the ideals of the American creed, limiting the promise of equality and justice only to members of the white race, and consistently behaves in ways that are consistent with such convictions. Members of white supremacist organizations such as the Ku Klux Klan or the Aryan Nations are explicit—and dangerous—examples of the All-Weather Illiberal. But one doesn't have to be a racist activist to fall into this category. Thus, the person who leaves a church that admits a black member or puts a for sale sign in the front yard of their home the moment a Jew moves into the neighborhood are examples of this type. Like the All-Weather Liberal, people fitting into this type exhibit consistency between beliefs and actions.

THE FAIR-WEATHER LIBERAL

Beyond these two types are individuals for whom prejudice and discrimination do, in fact, vary independently of each other. The first of these is the unprejudiced discriminator, whom Merton defines as a Fair Weather Liberal. These individuals believe in the American creed, yet choose to discriminate for reasons of convenience, ease, or profit. While they are not prejudiced in nature, they are prepared to discriminate against others either for their own benefit or in order to conform to the expectations of significant others in their lives. Merton cites as an example the employer who is neither anti-black nor anti-Semitic, but refuses to hire blacks and Jews because of a concern that "it might hurt business" (Merton 1949: 106).

THE FAIR-WEATHER ILLIBERAL

The prejudiced non-discriminator, on the other hand, does not believe in the American creed and holds prejudicial beliefs, yet does not practice discrimination. This type would characterize the employer who harbors prejudicial attitudes towards blacks and Jews, but hires them anyway. What would motivate a person to act in such a fashion? A major factor at play is fear of repercussions or consequences of discriminatory behavior. What might such an employer be afraid of? Since the passage of the landmark Civil Rights Act of 1964, such employers have often had reason to be afraid of the enforcement powers of the Equal Employment Opportunities Office of the Department of Justice and the threat of class-action lawsuits. This is the Fair-Weather Illiberal, a person that can be held to a position of non-discrimination through the enforcement of civil rights laws and social pressure. Similar to the Fair Weather Liberal, the behaviors of these individuals are driven by convenience, ease, and the path of least resistance. The lack of discrimination by the Fair Weather Illiberal is fragile, it goes against their own prejudicial beliefs, yet can be maintained through practice if it is clear that forces in the larger society stress that they are opposed to discriminatory conduct.

POLICY IMPLICATIONS

These last two types were important for Merton as he considered what the most effective social policies aimed at combating discrimination might be. He was writing just as the impact of the civil rights movement was about to be felt. Merton (1949: 111) asked where it would be possible to most effectively enact policies aimed at progressive social change, that is, "positive action for the reduction of ethnic discrimination." The typology allowed Merton to realize that these intermediate groups were the places where the greatest potential for change through the implementation of social policies was possible. Rather than trying to change the All-Weather Illiberal, who holds strong prejudicial beliefs and discriminates in practice, Merton suggests ways that social policy could be used to shift the types in the middle to reduce racial and ethnic discrimination. The Fair-Weather Liberal would benefit by refusing to discriminate because such a person would no longer feel the guilt and shame that often accompanies acts of discrimination. The Fair-Weather Illiberal, meanwhile, presents a more complicated case. Here policies aimed at reducing discrimination, if sufficiently strict and efficient, could reasonably be assumed to reduce levels of discrimination. Whether it would change the hearts-and-minds of such illiberals is another question. It might, Merton realized (1949: 118), actually result, at least in the short term, in increasing levels of prejudice.

PREJUDICE AS A SENSE OF GROUP POSITION

In what was an effort to offer a sharp contrast to Allport's social psychological work on prejudice, Herbert Blumer, who taught at both the University of Chicago and the University of California at Berkeley, offered a counterargument that claimed that prejudice could be better understood if it was treated in terms of what he describes as a sense of group position. In making this claim, he was asserting that sociology could offer insights about the nature of prejudice that were not possible by remaining rooted in psychological accounts. Although his specific focus is on race, his argument is applicable to intergroup relations for all ethnic groups.

A SOCIOLOGICAL APPROACH

"Race Prejudice as a Sense of Group Position" was published in 1958 in the inaugural issue of *The Pacific Sociological Review*. This brief article, amounting to only five pages of text, outlines Blumer's approach to the study of race prejudice as a sense of group position, or group position theory. Blumer (1958: 3) lays out his case in the following passage:

> In this paper I am proposing an approach to the study of race prejudice different from that which dominates contemporary scholarly thought on this topic. My thesis is that race prejudice exists basically in a sense of group position rather than in a set of feelings which members of one racial group have toward the members of another racial group. This different way of viewing race prejudice shifts study and analysis from a preoccupation with feelings lodged in individuals to a concern with the relationship of racial groups. It also shifts scholarly treatment away from individual lines of experience and focuses interest on the collective process by which a racial group comes to define and redefine another racial group. Such shifts, I believe, will yield a more realistic and penetrating understanding of race prejudice.

Blumer's approach was a direct response to work on prejudice at the time which focused on the individual. He insisted that we must look beyond the individual and explore the role of groups, institutions, and social structures if we are to succeed in understanding the nature of prejudice or, more broadly, race relations. As Blumer (1958: 3) stated in reaction to the individualistic approach characteristic of psychological theories, "Unfortunately, this customary way of viewing race prejudice overlooks and obscures the fact that race prejudice is fundamentally a matter of relationship between racial groups."

RACIAL DOMINATION

An underlying assumption that informs Blumer's thesis is that wherever one finds societies characterized by racial divisions, you will also find a racial hierarchy that is the product of historical forces, the outcome of which leads to racial domination of one group and the subordination of the other. The term "racial domination" is widely used in contemporary critical race theories, and in this regard Blumer can be appropriately seen as a precursor to such approaches.

Blumer (1958: 4) proceeded to describe four basic and interrelated types of feelings that he argues are always present in the racial prejudices of the dominant group: (1) feelings of superiority; (2) feeling that the subordinate race is intrinsically different and alien;

(3) feelings of proprietary claims to certain areas of privilege and advantage; and (4) fear and suspicion that the subordinate race harbors designs on the prerogatives of the dominant race.

Laid out in a simple and straightforward fashion, these four aspects of prejudice have offered subsequent scholars with a toolkit that has helped us to better understand how race relations operate in any society. As will be seen later in this chapter, the feeling of superiority is related to work in the race and ethnicity literature that focuses on the belief that blacks violate core American values (present in **symbolic racism** and **laissez-faire racism**) and are associated with negative stereotypes such as laziness and a lack of morals.

The feeling that the subordinate race is different and alien ties to work that has examined boundaries and otherness. In recent years a number of scholars have turned their attention to the topic of boundaries, including Michele Lamont and Virag Molnar (2002), Andreas Wimmer (2008), and Richard Alba (2010). It can also be seen in such studies as *Imperial Leather: Race, Gender and Sexuality in the Colonial Contest* by Anne McClintock (1995) and *Orientalism* Edward Said's (1979) now classic work.

A concern with the third feeling Blumer describes, having a proprietary claim to certain areas of privilege and advantage, is evident in recent work on whiteness and **white privilege**. This is a topic we'll discuss later in this chapter.

After describing these first three feelings, he points out that these three feelings either separately or in tandem cannot explain race prejudice. As Blumer (1958: 4) put it:

> These three feelings are present frequently in societies showing no prejudice, as in certain forms of feudalism, in caste relations, in societies of chiefs and commoners, and under many settled relations of conquerors and conquered. Where claims are solidified into a structure which is accepted or respected by all, there seems to be no group prejudice. The remaining feeling essential to race prejudice is a fear or apprehension that the subordinate racial group is threatening, or will threaten, the position of the dominant group.

With the addition of this fourth type of feeling, Blumer has foreshadowed work on group threat and contact theory (Blalock 1967; Quillian 1995, 1996). It is here especially that one finds a focus on the potential for conflict and violence, for when subordinates are viewed as a threat to the established racial hierarchy, the superordinate group's typical emotions are intensely negative, as apprehension mixes with covert or overt hostility.

In describing the typical feelings that can be expected to be present in the dominant group, Blumer is careful to point out that this is not to say the feelings and beliefs of the dominant group are homogenous and uniform across the group, for there can be considerable individual variation. In stressing this fact, he attempts to establish the idea that independent of individual beliefs or attitudes, the dominant group can maintain its position and privilege, even when individual members do not subscribe to these beliefs.

In studying issues of prejudice and racism, a considerable amount of time is often spent attempting to identify if individuals are racist or not, or harbor negative attitudes about other racial groups. Blumer's thesis about the privileged position of the dominant racial group mirrors more recent arguments that suggest that racial domination can continue to sustain itself even without individual racists, in the traditional sense (see Bonilla-Silva 2001 for an example of this same idea).

PSYCHOLOGY OR SOCIOLOGY

While we believe that Blumer has in retrospect played a major role in informing and providing insights that inform contemporary theories of prejudice, we do not think it necessary to attempt to separate psychology and sociology the way he set out to do. In fact, he didn't actually succeed in divorcing his position from psychology insofar as feelings, though socially constructed, inevitably can be viewed as psychological phenomena. In short, we would contend that the most productive way forward builds on the insights derived both from psychology and from sociology, and moreover that the most promising way to proceed is to encourage an interdisciplinary approach.

CONTEMPORARY CONCEPTUAL DEVELOPMENTS

In recent years, a major component of research on prejudice and discrimination has focused on racial attitudes and beliefs, as well as a concern with public opinion, especially about policies designed to combat prejudice and discrimination. Much of this work can be seen as representing either sociopsychological theories or political theories. In both instances, the imprint of earlier scholars, be it implicit or explicit, is evident. One additional branch of research can be classified as social structural theories (e.g., Sears, et al. 2000), which rather clearly can trace their origins to the work of Herbert Blumer. The following sections will examine these three theoretical approaches. It should be noted that whereas the classic statements were articulated before or during the early phase of the US civil rights movement, the theories we now turn to were formulated in the post-civil rights era, when the nation had entered into a new and uncertain race relations future. The final sections of this chapter discuss possibilities for the future of racial attitudes research, suggesting that a turn to whiteness and critical race theory may allow this research to build upon previous work and advance the field in new and productive directions.

SYMBOLIC RACISM AND SOCIOPSYCHOLOGICAL MODELS

At the core of sociopsychological models one finds the centrality of the concept known as symbolic racism, a concept that views racism today as different from "traditional racism" but still sees the role of individual racist attitudes as central in explaining racial attitudes and support (or lack thereof) for various public policies intended to combat prejudice and discrimination. Symbolic racism is based in approaches rooted in sociocultural learning and early-learned prejudice theories. The psychological underpinning of this concept is heavily influenced by the work of Allport.

While there are some elements of broader social and structural components contained in the theory, the role of individual beliefs at a psychological level is central. The seminal work in setting the parameters of what symbolic racism means is Donald Kinder and David Sears' article "Prejudice and Politics: Symbolic Racism versus Racial Threats to the Good Life" (1981). Kinder and Sears define symbolic racism as the combination of anti-black affect plus traditional American moral values. They describe these moral values as the Protestant ethic, which constitutes a misunderstanding of what Weber meant by that term. A better term would be the work ethic, which is in fact a term they also use.

Symbolic racism is rooted in deep-seated belief that blacks are hostile to basic American values, particularly those rooted in the Protestant or work ethic that stress individual self-reliance, hard work, self-restraint, and conformity to existing norms and laws (Kinder and Sears 1981: 416). The concept contains two key components. While a sense that blacks violate core American values is important, the concept of symbolic racism also requires a substantial level of anti-black affect. Kinder and Sears see these two components in combination as adding up to a persuasive explanation for contemporary racial attitudes. They used this theoretical framework to explain voting behavior in mayoral elections in Los Angeles in 1969 and 1973, which were elections where Tom Bradley, an African American politician, ran for office. Bradley's defeat in the 1969 Los Angeles mayoral election resulted in the widespread use of the term "the Bradley Effect" by political pundits and journalists. The idea of the Bradley Effect has been discussed frequently ever since, including during the 2008 Presidential election, which led to Barack Obama's electoral victory.

Back in 1969 many polls showed Bradley with a considerable lead as the election was approaching. However, his white opponent, Sam Yorty, won the election. Some analysts concluded that white voters told pollsters they would vote for Bradley before the election, but then voted instead for the white candidate when they entered the privacy of the voting booth. Why would they do so? One possibility was that anti-black attitudes remained common among a large segment of white voters, but they were hesitant to make those views public. Thus, their answer to pollsters was designed to indicate that they were not racist, while their voting behavior revealed that race did, indeed, play a large role in their decision. Four years later Bradley actually won the mayoral race. These two racially charged mayoral races served as a strategic research site for the initial development of the idea of symbolic racism.

RACIAL RESENTMENT

Over the next three decades, the concept was revised on several occasions in response to challenges posed by critics. In 1996, Donald Kinder and Lynn Sanders published *Divided by Color: Racial Politics and Democratic Ideals*, which is at once a continuation of the earlier work produced within the symbolic racism framework and an abandonment of the term. Instead of symbolic racism, they suggested that a more useful term is "racial resentment." Part of the reason for the introduction of the new term was a conscious decision to remove the word "racism" from the term since it had led to misinterpretations (Kinder and Sanders 1996: 292–293). So what is racial resentment and how is it different from the original concept?

Kinder and Sanders (1996: 36) began by listing what they believe are the three primary ingredients for understanding American public opinion on any issue: (1) the material interests at stake; (2) sympathy or resentment toward social groups in dispute; and (3) political principles. The material interests at stake are those systems and structures involved in political initiatives and votes on such racially sensitive topics as affirmative action, admissions in education, welfare, etc. What Kinder and Sanders found is that the role of material interests operates largely at a group-level, that of a perceived advantage or disadvantage to whites as a group, for example, rather than to one's own personal interests. They also see material interests in these cases being more about perceived threat than realistic threat or group conflict (Kinder and Sanders 1996: 88–91).

The other two ingredients in their recipe for understanding public opinion, sympathy or resentment toward social groups in dispute and political principles align with the original concept of symbolic racism very closely. Racial resentment is "a combination of racial anger and indignation, on the one hand, and a secularized version of the Protestant Ethic, on the other." (Kinder and Sanders 1996: 294). As we can see here, the central role of traditional American values is the same for symbolic racism and racial resentment. The largest difference between the two theoretical frameworks is the emotional, or attitudinal, element of the frames. Symbolic racism includes "anti-black affect" whereas racial resentment includes "racial anger and indignation." For symbolic racism, anti-black affect is the component of the term based in early-learning and prejudice, whereas for racial resentment, the anti-black component shifts from negative feelings against blacks stemming from early life phases to a more direct indignation, a feeling that "blacks do not try hard enough to overcome the difficulties they face and that they take what they have not earned" (Kinder and Sanders 1996: 106). In other words, whereas the cause in the older frame is rooted in the psychological imprint of the past, the new frame emphasizes the causal role of the contemporary context of race relations.

OTHER SOCIOPSYCHOLOGICAL CONCEPTS

These two concepts have been widely used by race relations scholars. But these are not the only terms that have gained currency. There are several other social psychological frameworks that fall within the sociopsychological category, including aversive racism, modern racism, and **subtle racism**. Aversive racism was developed conceptually by social psychologists and is based in the idea that whites avoid (are averse to) any awareness or recognition of their own negative attitudes toward African Americans. In fact, whites may overly emphasize the ways in which they feel they are exhibiting positive racial behaviors to minimize any potential perceived negative racial prejudices (Gaertner and Dovidio 1986). Modern racism is similar to symbolic racism in many ways but is distinctive insofar as it also pays particular attention to affective and cognitive components of racism as well as individual dynamics and behaviors (McConahay 1986). Subtle racism was a concept developed by Thomas Pettigrew and Roel Meertens to explain the prejudice they saw in Europe— prejudice that they concluded was different from blatant, overt, or traditional prejudice. While subtle racism also overlaps significantly with other social psychological theories of racial attitudes, it is unique in that it is primarily focused on prejudice in Western Europe, which is often the product of religious differences rather than racial differences. Pettigrew and Meertens used the Eurobarometer as their main data source. The notion of subtle racism is based on the assumption that prejudice is directed against outgroups in general, rather than against one particular group. It thus offers a broader scope than similar theories in the United States, which are primarily focused on white prejudice against blacks. (Pettigrew and Meertens 1995).

Critics of symbolic racism have raised concerns about its theoretical approach, concentrating their critiques in two main areas. First, some have argued that it is not substantially different from traditional, overt forms of racism and prejudice and that there may be some inconsistency in how the concept has been operationalized (e.g., Sniderman and Tetlock 1986). The second main area of criticism has focused on symbolic racism's treatment of group conflict. Some scholars argue that continued negative racial beliefs and actions can be better understood as based in self-interest and group conflict rather than prejudice.

POLITICAL THEORIES

Political theories of racial attitudes have not proven to be as central and prominent in much of the racial attitudes literature as other frameworks, although this work has garnered a large amount of attention in recent years. Indeed, as shall become evident, the work has proven to be quite controversial and has elicited polemical claims and counterclaims.

SNIDERMAN AND COLLEAGUES

In this section, the discussion of political theories of racial attitudes research focuses on research conducted by Paul Sniderman and various colleagues. This is not to say that there are not other significant theoretical contributions to the intersections of race and politics, but that these other works are beyond the scope of the general discussion here about racial attitudes research. Two books, *The Scar of Race* (1993), coauthored with Thomas Piazza, and *Reaching beyond Race* (1997), coauthored with Edward Carmines, are the most well-known works produced by Sniderman and his coauthors. In them, the authors offer critiques of much of the research on racial attitudes and provide an alternative way to think about racial attitudes and their impact on public policy. At its core, this work taken as a whole argues that views concerning social policies are not really about race. This is a sentiment that resonates with many people in America (and elsewhere) today who want to believe we have become a color-blind society that has at long last gotten past race.

Specifically, Sniderman and associates argue that opposition to US public policies designed to aid minorities and promote racial equality is not racist. Rather, the opposition stems from beliefs that these public policies violate traditional American values. Recall that the combination of racist beliefs and commitment to traditional American values is a core component of much of the recent work discussed previously. In contrast, Sniderman and his colleagues remove the racist beliefs component and argue that it is simply an issue of perceived violations of egalitarian beliefs and values, without racist foundations or implications.

The position of Sniderman and his colleagues is clear in the opening pages of *Reaching beyond Race*. Sniderman and Carmines (1997: 7) write that,

> Judged by the objective evidence, the overall impact of racial prejudice on the political choices that white Americans make turns out to be surprisingly modest ... The conclusion to draw is now clear: racial prejudice is not the dominant reason for the resistance of white Americans to current policies intended to help black Americans.

This assertion represents a major shift in thinking about the nature of racial attitudes. These authors argue that racial prejudice no longer plays a major role in explaining white Americans' resistance to race-based policies.

The empirical evidence the authors provide supports this position. In both books, data from telephone surveys are central to their argument. The research is tied to the "Race and Politics Studies" completed by the Survey Research Center at the University of California, Berkeley. These national studies were completed using CATI (computer assisted telephone interviewing). The studies took full advantage of the capabilities of CATI. A key feature of this research that made it distinctive was that it included several experiments in each survey. Sniderman and his colleagues argued that these experiments make a strong case that they are correct in their claim that racial prejudice and racial attitudes are not the main causes of white opposition to race-targeted public policies in America. In fact, these authors believe that whites would support policies designed to help and aid minorities if politicians would approach these issues in a new way. There is no need to change what people think and believe. Rather it's necessary to change the language used in framing policies. Specifically, they endorse the idea of replacing the particularistic language of race-specific policies with an argument based on "universal principles that reach beyond race" (Sniderman and Carmines 1997: 8).

Critics of this research have argued that the experiments are not as powerful and conclusive as they believe. For example, Howard Schuman and coauthors (1997: 369–370) contend that,

> Sniderman and his colleagues tend to treat randomized experiments as more definitive than they can ever be, for example, claiming in one case that a single experiment of theirs produced results that "exploded the notion that whites will say what they believe they are supposed to say about matters of race."

THE "MERE MENTION" EXPERIMENT

Additionally, the explanatory power of the experiments presented by Sniderman and others is often subject to interpretation of the results of the experiments themselves. The evidence Sniderman and his colleagues provide is based on their understanding of the data from the experiments, not simply based on the data themselves. For example, Sniderman and Carmines' use the "Mere Mention" experiment to show that "the mere mention of affirmative action turns out to sharpen hostility to blacks." (1997: 40). They argue that white Americans' dislike for affirmative action is so strong that it actually increases negative feelings towards those who benefit from their program. Essentially, they have reversed the more typical causal argument. Instead of arguing that negative feelings toward blacks causes whites to oppose affirmative action, Sniderman and Carmines argue the opposite, that negative feelings toward affirmative action causes whites to have negative feelings about blacks. Their claim is "proven" by the "Mere Mention" experiment. In this experiment, half of the respondents are first asked to describe what blacks are like and then are asked their views of affirmative action. The other half of respondents are first asked their views of affirmative action and then are asked to describe what blacks are like. The data from this experiment showed that, "Whites who have just been asked to give an opinion about affirmative action are significantly more likely to describe 'most blacks' as 'lazy' than are whites to whom affirmative action has not been mentioned" (Sniderman and Carmines 1997: 39).

This is the empirical data from their experiment. However, the power of this data comes from their interpretation of the experiment, not from the data. Sniderman and Carmines claim that this experiment shows that whites have a problem with affirmative action, not blacks. However, it is just as plausible that whites have negative attitudes about blacks and that mentioning affirmative action first merely brings these negative attitudes about blacks to the forefront, so that they respond more negatively to the following question when asked to describe blacks. Given that affirmative action is generally associated with blacks, people may not be able to distinguish the policy from the intended recipient. Who is right? There is no way to know which interpretation is correct by simply looking at the data. Both explanations are plausible and possible. Yet Sniderman and Carmines' thesis rests on their interpretation of this experiment, even though they provide no compelling reason to believe their interpretation is more accurate than alternatives.

It is interesting to note that Sniderman has, with Dutch colleague Louk Hagendoorn, produced a parallel argument about **multiculturalism** and Muslims in the Netherlands, arguing that Dutch citizens were opposed to multiculturalism because of its presumed lack of congruence with cherished liberal values of individualism and tolerance, but were not hostile to Muslims as people or to Islam. Not surprisingly, the same criticisms of the work noted above is applicable here (Sniderman and Hagendoorn 2009).

THE CRITICS' CASE

Throughout *The Scar of Race* and *Reaching beyond Race*, experiment after experiment is presented. Each experiment and the empirical results are described in great detail, yet their interpretations and conclusions are simply stated, with little backing or reason to believe their conclusions above all others. This is arguably a case of strong empirical evidence coupled with weak interpretations.

The weak interpretations offered by Sniderman and his colleagues may also be the result of a lack of a theoretical framework underpinning their research. In contrast to much of the other work in racial attitudes research, there is a not an underlying theoretical framework within which their work is situated. The work does not begin with a theory or a set of assumptions about the world they study. This lack of theory is noted by Pettigrew and Meertens (2001: 299) in their critique of this approach and simultaneous defense of their own research:

> [Sniderman *et al.*] demonstrate that, if (a) you have no theory, (b) use different methods, and (c) make different assumptions, you can produce an analysis of prejudice different from ours ... We do not find this surprising. Nor do we see any reason to withdraw our claims for both the concept and measurement of subtle prejudice.

POLITICAL IMPLICATIONS

The importance of describing the criticisms of this particular brand of political theory about racial attitudes here is based in the fact that these theories are very appealing to many people today, especially in an era that some would like to call a new "post-racial era." The conclusion that derives from Sniderman and his colleagues is that whites in America are no longer racist, that the "race problem" should be viewed as a thing of the past. It is becoming more and more common to hear claims of living in a post-racial, color-blind society. While this work supports these claims in many ways, it is important to recognize that many scholars see flaws and fundamental shortcomings with research produced by this approach.

A final criticism is that it appears to many that the motivation for this line of research may be primarily to prove that whites are not racist, and more specifically that white conservatives are not more racist than other groups of whites. It is true that no social scientist comes at their research with a purely objective mind without any preconceived notions about what they may find. However, critics contend that Sniderman and his colleagues' motivations and intent seem arguably more transparent than others in the field of racial attitudes research.

CRITIQUING THE CRITICS

Sniderman and Tetlock (1986) have responded to criticisms with a critique of their own, placing particular focus on symbolic racism. They find the use of this influential concept troubling because, they contend, it suffers from a number of serious problems, including methodological issues, empirical shortcomings, and theoretical imprecision. They present a very vigorous attack on the idea of symbolic racism. More specifically, they claim that proponents of symbolic racism have unnecessarily politicized research agendas by treating opposition to race-based governmental programs as inherently racist. One of the results of this approach is to view conservatives as more racist than the rest of the population due to their hostility to a range of race-specific governmental programs.

Critics characterized this assessment as a misguided interpretation: to say that a major function of symbolic racism is to identify people who dislike blacks as primarily conservative. What is clear is that Sniderman and his associates are preoccupied with the idea that someone will be mistakenly called a racist. They suspect that symbolic racism is designed to be a tool that can "out" racists and that it might "out" people who are not really racists. From their perspective, there are fewer people who are racist than symbolic racism theorists claim and, moreover, the relationship between racism and conservatism is weaker than they claim as well. It is true that a central argument advanced by practitioners of the symbolic racism model is that contemporary racial prejudice is linked to conservative political values (Kinder and Sears 1981). It is similarly true that a driving force behind the entire line of research developed and forwarded by Sniderman and his colleagues represents a sustained attempt to dissolve this link between conservatism and racism.

Supporters of this line of research see this work as an important voice added to the dialogue about race in America. There is a feeling that Sniderman and others are finally saying what regular Americans have known for some time. It is perceived as a backlash against academic liberals and elites who overemphasize race. The back cover of *The Scar of Race* includes a quote from neoconservative intellectual Abigail Thernstrom, which reads:

> Lots of ordinary folks know it, but it's not the sort of thing social scientists tend to say: When it comes to questions of public policy, few whites are racists. Whites may oppose particular items on the standard civil rights agenda, but they're not bigots. That's the main point in *The Scar of Race* and it's a stinging rebuke to the cultural elite that generally thinks otherwise.

POLICY IMPLICATIONS

The appeal of this argument for many is that it claims that whites are increasingly free from racist bias and that prejudice and discrimination are not the primary causes of the existing racial inequality in America. In *Reaching beyond Race*, Sniderman and Carmines argue for universal, **color-blind policies** designed to help all who need assistance instead of racially targeted programs. They believe the only way to redress existing inequalities is to create a coalition of Americans, white and black, that is based on moral principles beyond race.

This call for universalistic programs parallels to some extent the argument advanced by William Julius Wilson (1987) on behalf of "Universal Programs of Reform." Both believe that a genuinely equal opportunity society will only be possible when the nation promotes programs designed to help all those in need, regardless of race. However, the differences are also significant. Wilson, advocating a social democratic vision, was explicit that class differences were playing an increasing role in shaping black life chances, and it was his focus on the intersection of class and race and his sense that class was becoming more significant for blacks led to his embrace of universal entitlement programs. However, it is worth noting that he later concluded that such programs needed to exist side-by-side with race-targeted programs, not as an alternative to them (Wilson 1999).

Can race-neutral, color-blind policies truly overcome the racial inequality that is present in our society today? Eduardo Bonilla-Silva and Tyrone Foreman don't think so. They conducted interviews with college students and did not find support for color-blind policies. In fact, they found that "virtually no policy alternatives were envisioned as feasible for addressing the profound inequality existing between Blacks and Whites. This casts serious doubt on arguments that suggest class-based or color-blind policies can unite whites and racial minorities" (Bonilla-Silva and Foreman 2000: 77). In his book, *White Supremacy and Racism in the Post-Civil Rights Era*, Bonilla-Silva (2001: 137) argues that color-blind racism, his term for racism in the post-civil rights era, "has emerged to support and reproduce the new racial structure of the United States." Universalistic policies, purporting to be race-neutral, can be conceived of as variations of color-blind racism. The danger is that by removing race from the discussion, claiming we now live in a post-race era, and removing racial aspects from policies designed to help disadvantaged people in our society, it becomes nearly impossible to continue to talk about race or continued racial inequality. In this approach, race itself is removed from the conversation. Bonilla-Silva argues that this approach can be a tool for whites, in a collective position of power, to maintain their position.

Increasingly, whites object to those who "always bringing race" into the discussion and get frustrated that minorities are too ready to "play the race card." Bonilla-Silva argues that the ideology (and power) of a post-race, color-blind ideology is clear in these situations, contending that a focus on universal policies for equality and opportunity for all may sound good in theory, but in reality, it may simply silence discussions about race and hide existing racial inequalities.

SOCIAL STRUCTURAL THEORIES

As mentioned earlier in this chapter, social structural theories of racial attitudes primarily build upon Blumer's group position theory rather than traditional work on prejudice and discrimination associated with the psychological approach of Allport. This difference in underlying theoretical foundations results in a very different trajectory and focus in the research—both in terms of the nature and significance of racial attitudes as well as assessments of the enduring legacy of prejudice and discrimination. The major ideas within social structural theories of racial attitudes are discussed below.

LAISSEZ-FAIRE RACISM

Laissez-faire racism represents an alternative theoretical framework to social psychological theoretical explanations of racial attitudes, including symbolic racism. It has proven to be another influential attempt to understand racial attitudes in the post-civil rights era. In a seminal article, Larry Bobo and Ryan Smith (1998) mapped out the characteristics and origins of laissez-faire racism, which they see as a replacement for **Jim Crow** racism—the racism characteristic of the period from the end of Reconstruction to the civil right movement. Whereas Jim Crow racism was based in a belief in black biological inferiority, laissez-faire racism is predicated on notions of black cultural inferiority. Bobo, the key spokesperson for this position, and his colleagues, contend that ideological justifications of racial inequalities based on biological inferiority have largely faded away in recent decades. They have been replaced by cultural justifications. While it is no longer acceptable in most social settings to assert that blacks are biologically inferior, cultural explanations bringing in factors such as family-upbringing and values are quite commonplace today.

Also central to the theory of laissez-faire racism is an active resistance to change in the racial order. As Bobo and Smith (1998: 186) put it, "Laissez-faire racism blames blacks themselves for the black-white gap in socioeconomic standing and actively resists meaningful efforts to ameliorate America's racist social conditions and institutions." This second part of the definition of laissez-faire racism is important insofar as it takes the concept further than simply being a set of explanations and justifications for racial inequality. It posits that laissez-faire racism is implicated in actively maintaining the current racial order and hierarchy. This theory suggests that continued racial prejudice and inequality is not simply an unfortunate consequence of psychological traits, but rather that there are structural forces at play that reinforce racial both racial attitudes and patterns of durable inequality.

Laissez-faire racism is very explicitly based on Blumer's notion of group position. It is an attempt to shift the focus from individual attitudes to group position, relative status, and the racial hierarchy. Prejudice, thus, is defined as a sense of group position. The hierarchical relationship between groups in society is part of the basis for prejudice, rather than being solely based on individual feelings and beliefs. This focus on group position offers laissez-faire racism a more structural understanding than one finds in sociopsychological theories. Bobo and Smith (1998: 187) are clear that this was their intent when they wrote that, "The framework takes seriously the imperatives deriving from the institutionalized structural social conditions of social life." The authors go on to emphasize their different level of focus compared to social psychological theories by writing:

> The theory of Laissez-Faire Racism, as we develop it here, focuses principally on predominant social patterns. These patterns are an aggregation of individual views, to be sure. Yet our main concern is not with variation in the attitudes of individuals but with the common or general pattern of thoughts, feelings, and beliefs about blacks. In that sense, we seek to characterize the current historical epoch, not simply or mainly to explain the distribution and effects of the attitudes of individuals
>
> (Bobo and Smith 1998: 187)

Another distinctive feature of laissez-faire racism is that it contains a historical dimension. Rather than assuming that racism is an ahistorical phenomenon, such that racism in the nineteenth century is the same as that in the twentieth, the concept is predicated on the notion that the shift from one epoch to another spells changes in the nature and dynamics of racism. The shift from Jim Crow racism to laissez-faire racism recognizes that the society after the civil rights movement is different from the society before the movement. Scholars agree that there have been significant positive shifts in racial attitudes, as reflected in public opinion survey questions asked repeatedly over the past several decades, such as the changing attitudes regarding black/white intermarriage reported in Figure 2.1. The positive shifts in attitudes are largely the reason for concluding that traditional, blatant, Jim Crow racism has indeed declined.

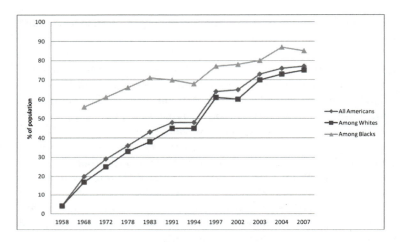

Figure 2.1: Approval of black/white marriages.

Bobo and Smith take this a step further by actually showing how Jim Crow racism declined and then showing how laissez-faire racism emerged. They do this by examining significant events that occurred in American society throughout much of the twentieth century. Of particular salience were political and economic changes that undercut the tradition form of tenant farming in the South. They also took into account the system of legal segregation during the Jim Crow era, the impact of the civil rights movement in ending that system, the growing resources available for blacks as they engaged in collective action, and the decline in the importance of cotton in the country's evolving economy.

DOMINANT IDEOLOGY

The concept of dominant ideology is most often associated with James Kluegel and Eliot Smith, especially as it was developed in *Beliefs about Inequality: Americans' Views of What Is and What Ought to Be* (1986). This book contains a theoretical framework that is very similar to other social structural theories, yet unfortunately this book rarely gets more than a citation in recent articles on racial attitudes. The authors discuss two key concepts that they use to explain current attitudes about economic inequality and policies. They are "dominant ideology" and "social liberalism." The dominant ideology is similar to the concepts of American individualism, the Protestant Ethic, traditional American values, etc. Kluegel and Smith (1986: 5) describe the dominant ideology as the idea that,

> opportunity for economic advancement based on hard work is plentiful ... [and] Individuals are personally responsible for their own economic fate ... As a consequence, since individual outcomes are proportional to individual inputs (talent and effort), the resulting unequal distribution of economic rewards is, in the aggregate, equitable and fair.

This concept resonates with other theoretical frameworks. If opportunities abound and anyone who tries hard enough can succeed, then those that have not succeeded are clearly personally responsible. It is generally known that at the societal level, African Americans and other minorities are not as economically successful as whites. What Kluegel and Smith tell us by using the concept of dominant ideology is that a common rationalization for these inequalities is adherence to traditional American values of individualism and hard work. Those that do not succeed have not taken advantage of the opportunities they have been given. This rationalization entirely overlooks structural forces working against groups of people in the United States. It also ignores the continuing impact of history. However, as all these authors point out, these core values of individual effort and achievement are so central, deep, and long-standing in American society that they can easily play a critical role in justifying, explaining, and defending the stark inequalities that persist.

Kluegel and Smith also employ the concept of social liberalism to explain current attitudes about inequalities. Social liberalism goes hand in hand with the dominant ideology thesis in explaining modern racial attitudes. Social liberalism entails the "acceptance of social and political equity with groups such as blacks and women, without the bases of economic inequality being called into question" (Kluegel and Smith 1986: 5–6). People (especially whites) at present generally believe in the virtue of social and political equality. The subtle, covert, modern forms of racism and prejudice become more complicated and ambiguous because of this. In theory and in abstract ways, there is a basic consensus that everyone should be treated as equals. Kluegel and Smith's use of social liberalism shows how this can be the case while commitment to the dominant ideology allows economic and material inequalities to continue to exist.

SOCIAL DOMINANCE THEORY

Social dominance theory begins with the claim that all human societies throughout time have been shaped by group-based hierarchies. All social systems consist of at least two unequal groups, a hegemonic group at the top and a negative reference group at the bottom (Sidanius, *et al.* 1992). According to this theory, dominance is a common element of all human cultures. There is always a dominant group and an oppressed group. These claims define the foundation of social dominance theory. Like laissez-faire racism, group position plays a key role here as well. However, social dominance theory starts from a much stronger position. The theory posits that social dominance is present and central to all societies—in other words, it is a universal given rather than a historically contingent fact. Racism in modern American society is just one case study of a larger trans-societal phenomenon.

Jim Sidanius is most often seen as the key spokesperson for this stance, having developed it in association with Felicia Pratto, Eric Devereux, and other coauthors. It is interesting to note that psychologists, and not sociologists, developed this theory. In some ways, social dominance theory contains elements of both social psychological theory and structural theory. Its psychological character is evident in its attention to individual behaviors. But its emphasis on hierarchy reflects a more sociological and structural approach, reminiscent of Blumer's group position theory.

It is important to understand that this theory does not simply end with the claim that all societies are defined by hierarchical systems. It goes further by describing how social hierarchies are actively maintained, reinforced, and reproduced. This emphasis on action and on the mechanisms of social construction and preservation strengthens the theory and its explanatory power in understanding societal-level discrimination and oppression. Its advocates focus on institutional discrimination and individual discrimination, but also include behavioral traits, bringing both the sociological and the psychological into their theoretical framework. The basic psychological assumption is that it is a natural, human tendency to view the group that one is a member of as in fundamental ways superior to other groups and as such deserving of higher status and various indicators of privilege. A problem with this approach is that it tends to essentialize group differences, and insofar as this is true, to view hierarchies as permanent and thus not amenable to change.

REIMAGINING RACIAL ATTITUDES FROM A WHITE PRIVILEGE PERSPECTIVE

Sociopsychological theories of racial attitudes look at individual's attitudes and beliefs about minority groups and their presumed values. More macro-level concepts regarding culture and social structural factors only come in to play insofar as they influence individual attributes and help explain personal behaviors. Social structural theories begin to bring into their frameworks an interest in culture, social systems, and institutions. By incorporating these concepts, it becomes easier to be critical of the existing system of racial inequality. Social Dominance Theory challenged the racial status quo and explicitly discussed racialized positions of domination and subordination in our society. However, while the theory began to incorporate power and domination into its framework, it still did not adequately discuss privilege itself and the life experiences of whites, the privileged or dominant group in the US. Social Dominance Theory overlooked important aspects of whites' own agency. In other words, while whites are in a dominant position, little attention is actually devoted to whites themselves, particularly the activities that they engage in that serve to maintain the existing racial hierarchy

This is the perspective that can be uncovered and subsequently incorporated into racial attitudes when the starting point is whiteness. Whites' material reality and life experiences need to be included in the analysis if we are to arrive at a comprehensive picture of race and racial attitudes in America. The vast majority of whites do not directly, explicitly, and with malice engage in conduct aimed at oppressing members of minority groups. Rather, they are ordinary, basically decent people who happen to enjoy lives of racial advantage and privilege, and thus confront far few barriers to success than their minority counterparts. They have a tendency to see their successes in terms of hard work, combined sometimes with a bit of luck, managing to be at the right place at the right time. This privilege is understood as a fortunate set of circumstances and events, not as a societal system of privilege designed to benefit whites.

Box 2.2: A personal example of white privilege.

Paul Croll describes his own encounter with white privilege in the following example:

I am white. A couple years ago, I got into a small automobile accident in my community in the Midwest United States. There was little damage to either car, but the police came to the scene. When the police arrived, I realized I did not have my current insurance card with me. According to state law, you have to have current insurance information in your vehicle at all times. I exchanged contact information with the other driver and then told the officer that I must have forgotten to put my new insurance card in my car. The officer told me not to worry about my lack of current insurance and sent me on my way.

Around the same time, a Latino student of mine was home over break. He had just bought a new car and was nervous he would get pulled over by the police. So he kept all the paperwork from the dealer on the front seat next to him and made sure he drove within the speed limit and did not break any traffic laws. Nonetheless, a police officer did pull him over. The officer did not say why he pulled him over, but asked why he only had one license plate on his car. State law requires all cars to have license plates on the front and back of the vehicles. The student explained it was a new car and that the dealer only gave him one temporary license plate. He showed the officer the paperwork and receipts from the dealer. The officer said, "Son, it is state law to have two plates on your car." The student tried to explain again that it was not his fault and that the dealer only gave him one plate. The officer responded by saying "Boy, are you trying to cause some trouble?" With that, the officer wrote him a ticket for only having one plate and left.

I broke the law. I was driving without insurance. My student was only given one temporary plate from the dealer. He did nothing wrong. Yet I walked away and my student got a ticket.

WHITENESS STUDIES

Whiteness studies constitute a specific type of critical race theory. Central to whiteness theory is the idea that racialized systems of power and domination have been normalized and hidden. Whiteness is also a cultural phenomenon wherein whites are not particularly cognizant of their own race, or of the racialized nature of their position in society. This work has been profoundly interdisciplinary in nature. The major works in whiteness studies come from academic fields as diverse as history, sociology, legal studies, literature, women's studies, and education.

Key works in history and critical race theory launched an awareness of whiteness in the late 1980s and early 1990s. Arguments from historians and historical sociologists led the way in showing the changing boundaries of white status with an emphasis on how European ethnics, chiefly from eastern and southern Europe "became" white over time, rather than being treated by the receiving society as "white on arrival." Historians such as David Roediger (2005) have contributed considerably to our understanding of the costs and consequences of these transformations for various groups, beginning with the Irish who were sometimes depicted as European counterparts to blacks. By the last decades of the century, recently arrived groups such as Poles, Italians, and Jews discovered that they were seen as "in-between peoples," not really black, but not quite white, either (Barrett and Roediger 1997; see also Jacobson 1998). In a broader sense, this historically oriented scholarship sought to make the point that whiteness is in fact part of a broader field of **racial formation** (Omi and Winant 1994).

More broadly, critical race theorists provided a lens by which to examine American institutions and values in a way that sheds light on their role in maintaining and reproducing racial inequality. Critical race theorists challenged the idea that principles such as liberalism and equal opportunity, both in the legal system and in broader society, necessarily and inevitably lead to racial justice and equality.

The late Ruth Frankenberg (1994: 1), one of the sociologists who pioneered work in the area of whiteness studies, described whiteness as a set of three linked dimensions.

> First, whiteness is a location of structural advantage, of race privilege. Second, it is a "standpoint," a place from which white people look at themselves and others, and at society. Third, "whiteness" refers to a set of cultural practices that are usually unmarked and unnamed.

Frankenburg's claims—that whiteness relates to both privilege and identity, and that it becomes normalized and invisible—summarize the main insights of this field of inquiry. Peggy McIntosh (1989: 10) reinforced this line of thinking in a widely cited description of white privilege as the "invisible weightless knapsack of special provisions, maps, passports, codebooks, visas, clothes, tools, and blank checks."

In short, the structural question of white privilege—its construction, its reproduction, indeed its very existence—is at the core of whiteness studies' contribution to sociological theories of race relations and racial inequalities.

CRITICAL THEORIES OF RACE

INSTITUTIONAL RACISM

One of the clearest examples of a critique of the role of race in American society during the post-civil rights era is found in the concept of institutional racism which covers similar terrain as work in whiteness studies, although it has evolved from a different theoretical origin. The idea of institutional racism came out of the 1960s' Black Power Movement. The term "institutional racism" was first developed by Stokley Carmichael and Charles Hamilton in their book, *Black Power* (1967: 4), which they explain in the following way:

> Racism is both overt and covert. It takes two, closely related forms: individual whites acting against individual blacks, and acts by the total white community against the black community. We call these individual racism and institutional racism. The first consists of overt acts by individuals, which causes death, injury or the violent destruction of property. This type can be recorded by television cameras; it can frequently be observed in the process of commission. The second type is less overt, far more subtle, and less identifiable in terms of *specific* individuals committing these acts. But it is no less destructive of human life. The second type originates in the operation of established and respected forces in society, and thus receives far less public condemnation than the first type.

A small number of race scholars have continued work within the framework of institutional racism. In *Systemic Racism: A Theory of Oppression* (2006) Joe Feagin developed these ideas further in his articulation of a theory of systemic racism. Barbara Trepagnier's recent book, *Silent Racism: How Well-Meaning White People Perpetuate the Racial Divide* (2010) similarly builds upon earlier formulations of institutional racism. It can be argued that institutional racism offers a way to conceive of racial inequality as a consequence of institutional factors in combination with individual factors. While it covers very similar terrain to whiteness studies, the two approaches to race relations have typically not been brought together for common purpose, although this has begun to change in recent years with work by Feagin (2001), Bonilla-Silva (2001, 2010), and Trepagnier (2010).

RACIAL FORMATIONS

Michael Omi and Howard Winant offer yet another critical examination of the racialized system in America. In *Racial Formation in the United States: From the 1960s to the 1990s* (1994), they developed the theory of racial formations (influenced by the Italian Marxist theorist, Antonio Gramsci), a theory which provides a way to think about the ongoing and contested social, economic and political processes that determine the meaning and content of racial categories and systems in society. Omi and Winant's focus on mechanisms and evolving racialized systems helps to uncover the often hidden processes at work that continue to maintain and reproduce racial inequality.

Winant uses the concept of racial formations in his later work to examine racial projects in the post-civil rights era. He argued that in the post-civil rights era

> monolithic white supremacy is over, yet in a more concealed way, white power and privilege live on... Whites are no longer the official "ruling race" yet they still enjoy many of the privileges descended from the time when they were
>
> (Winant 1997: 76)

While white power and privilege continue for Winant, he also explains how the ideology of color-blindness has also developed for many whites. While real gains in racial justice were achieved as a consequence of the civil rights movement, Winant argued that substantive equality did not emerge. He believes that real equality would have entailed a substantial redistribution of **income** and **wealth**, and associated structural change. As such, these changes would have constituted a threat to the interests of the capitalist class, and for this reason societal elites never sought to advance and were not prepared to permit substantive equality. However, a large enough number of whites believed that a reasonable level of equality had been achieved, so that race targeted social policies such as affirmative action were to be rejected in favor of what were seen as color-blind policies (Winant 1997).

COLOR-BLIND RACISM

The sociologist best known for continuing work on color-blind racism is Eduardo Bonilla-Silva. In his books, *White Supremacy and Racism in the Post-Civil Rights Era* (2001) and *Racism without Racists: Color-Blind Racism and the Persistence of Racial Inequality in the United States* (2010), he expands and develops the idea of color-blind racism and uses it to provide a critique of what he sees as American liberalism's failure to adequately address racism and racial inequality. Bonilla-Silva uses a combination of survey data and in-depth interviews—including the excerpt contained in Box 2.3—to explore empirically manifestations of color-blind racism and its implications for racial attitudes.

Box 2.3: Color-blind racism.

When thinking about contemporary racial inequality in the United States, Eduardo Bonilla-Silva asks the following questions:

How is it possible to have this tremendous degree of racial inequality in a country where most whites claim that race is no longer relevant? More important, how do whites explain the apparent contradiction between their professed color blindness and the United States' color-coded inequality? ... I contend that whites have developed powerful explanations – which have ultimately become justifications – for contemporary racial inequality that exculpate them from any responsibility for the status of people of color. These explanations emanate from a new racial ideology that I label color-blind racism.

(Bonilla Silva 2010: 2)

Bonilla-Silva conducted in-depth interviews with respondents to study the ideology of color-blind racism. Below are several examples of color-blind racism from his research:

> I don't think that they (minority students) should be provided with unique opportunities. I think that they should have the same opportunities as everyone else. You know, it's up to them to meet the standards and whatever that's required for entrance into universities or whatever, I don't think that just because they're a minority that they should, you know, not meet the requirements, you know.
>
> (Bonilla-Silva 2010: 31)

> Again, I don't think that we can make retribution for things that happened in the past. I don't think it serves any purpose today to try to fix something that happened a long time ago that doesn't affect anyone today. All it does is bring up to the surface that there was a problem.
>
> (Bonilla-Silva 2010: 78)

> No, and I, you know, I have to say that I'm pretty supportive of anything to help people, but I don't know why that slavery thing has a – I've got a chip on my shoulder about that. It's like it happened so long ago and you've got these sixteen year-old kids saying, "Well, I deserve because great, great granddaddy was a slave." Well, you know what, it doesn't affect you. Me, as a white person, I had nothing to do with slavery. You, as a black person, you never experienced it. It was so long ago I just don't see how that pertains to what's happening to the race today so, you know, that's one thing that I'm just like, "God shut up!"
>
> (Bonilla-Silva 2010: 80–81)

Bonilla-Silva argues that color-blind racism promotes "the idea that race has all but disappeared as a factor shaping the life chances of all Americans." (Bonilla-Silva 2010: 262). In a country where stark racial inequalities continue to persist, color-blind racism allows whites to claim that racism is a thing of the past and that opportunities are now open and equal for all.

Bonilla-Silva treats color-blind racism as consisting of four dominant frames: (1) abstract liberalism (a somewhat confusing term that refers to beliefs that merge extreme individualism with hostility to government intervention); (2) biologization of culture; (3) naturalization of racial matters; and (4) minimization of racism (Bonilla-Silva 2001: 141–142). Bonilla-Silva's use of abstract liberalism as a dominant frame of color-blind racism explicitly ties liberalism to color-blindness and shows how liberalism itself can play a role in maintaining and reproducing racial inequality. Bonilla-Silva combines many elements of whiteness, critical race theory, and institutional racism in his own theoretical formations. He has sought to explain how racial inequality and racial oppression can continue to exist without individual racists acting in acting in overtly discriminatory and exploitive ways.

CONCLUSION

This chapter surveyed the ways that sociologists and psychologists have sought to understand prejudice and discrimination. It set the stage by providing an overview of three classic figures in the field, two sociologists and one psychologist, who in various ways influenced subsequent work. The bulk of the chapter focused on contemporary approaches to racial attitudes, which we divided into three categories: social-psychological, political, and social structural. Two concepts that were created in order to understand the nature of racism in the post-civil rights era stood out insofar as they have proven to be widely accepted and used by a significant number of scholars in the field: symbolic racism and laissez-faire racism. The chapter concluded with a discussion of recent developments that have sought to refocus attention by examining white privilege and the way it is perpetuated today in a racial formation that has been characterized as being shaped by color-blind racism.

3

THE DYNAMICS OF INEQUALITY

Inequality exists in all societies, but it does not manifest itself in the same way everywhere and at all times. Among the major systems defining the unequal distribution of valued resources in any particular society are chattel slavery and caste systems at one end of the spectrum to social class systems at the other. Slavery has existed globally and continues to the present, particularly in various countries in Southeast Asia, the Indian subcontinent, Africa, and the Arab world (Bales 1999). In the older form of slavery—chattel slavery— one group of people owns not simply the labor of another, but actually owns that person. In the system of slavery in the United States which began in the seventeenth century and ended with the signing of the Emancipation Proclamation during the Civil War, the white plantation class owned African slaves. The slave trade ended early in the nineteenth century, but slavery was perpetuated for several more decades by enslaving the children of slaves. In the American South, as in other times and places, slavery was seen as natural and therefore just. This was seen elsewhere as well. In the case of Britain, slavery was outlawed before it was in the US, while in the case of Brazil, which imported more African slaves than any other country in the western hemisphere, slavery would not end until 1888.

Likewise, the idea that inequality is both natural and inevitable is associated with caste systems, where the social status of individuals is connected to their ritual purity or impurity. As with slavery, in a caste system there is no movement out of the status of one's birth. One of the most elaborate examples of a caste system can be found in India. Officially outlawed in 1950, the Indian caste system was supported by the Hindu concepts of karma and dharma. The Hindu religion believes that people experience several lifetimes, during which they suffer, until they achieve perfection. Karma was the belief that in this lifetime, a person is born into a particular caste—high or low—because she or he deserves to be there based on actions in a past life. Dharma refers to leading a moral existence in one's present life. Even the lowliest untouchable who lived with grace according to the rules of caste could be reborn into a higher caste. But this meant that upward mobility in a Hindu caste society could only occur in another lifetime. Both caste systems and slave systems prohibit mobility from one status group to another in this life.

In the American South, after the signing of the Emancipation Proclamation, the treaty ending the Civil War, and the upheaval that took place during the era of Reconstruction, some argue that a system of color caste replaced slavery. This was the era known as Jim Crow that arose gradually in the aftermath of the Civil War and persisted until the civil rights movement a century later (Fredrickson 2002; Dollard 1937). Another example of color caste was the apartheid system in South Africa noted in Chapter 1 wherein the society was divided among whites, coloreds (the term used to refer to mixed race peoples), Indians and Africans in a context where economic, political, and cultural control rested in the hands of the white minority, with the African majority leading impoverished and marginalized lives and the other two castes existing in the interstices between the black and white populations (Frederickson 2008: 137–169).

A third way of distributing valued resources which characterized premodern European history was feudalism, predicated on the division of society into estates. A system of inequality justified by early Christian theology, wealth was tied to ownership of the land. Stewardship of land in rural England, France, Italy and other countries was in the hands of a small minority of the population, including the members of the aristocracy and the church hierarchy. The vast majority of the population consisted of the impoverished peasantry, with a relatively small stratum of other economic sectors—including shop owners, petty government officials, intellectuals, and the like—rounding out the population as a whole. In the centuries before industrialization, a person's position in life was for the most part determined at birth. One was born into the landed aristocracy or born to work the land. In this world, the hegemonic aristocracy and the peasants were mutually dependent on each other. Peasants' lives depended on their ability to cultivate the land owned by their "lord," who in turn amassed wealth as a consequence of the system of unequal exchange that benefited the feudal lords at the expense of the peasants. Vast inequalities characterized this world. The extreme differences of wealth were justified by the belief that poverty could be ennobling and that members of each estate had a distinct contribution to make to maintain social order.

When industrialization replaced an economic system predicated on agricultural production and the ownership of land, beliefs about the proper distribution of valued resources began to be rethought. So did beliefs about the heretofore presumed natural and God-given character of a social order predicated on a hierarchal society that resembled a pyramid with the rich at the top and the poor at the bottom. The idea of one group being "naturally inferior" to another by birth was questioned, as was the idea that social mobility from one rank to another ought to be, if not prohibited, at least severely restricted. In this new industrial economy, caste gave way to social class, which should be understood as a social location in the economic order that can have both an ascribed and an achieved character. While at birth individuals acquire a class location predicated on the social class of their parents, the possibility exists—to exactly what extent being open to question—of moving from one class to another due to hard work, intellect, chance, or some combination thereof.

IS INEQUALITY BENEFICIAL TO THE WELL-BEING OF SOCIETY?

When there is evidence of greater economic mobility, and a sense that many people end up being better off than they once were, there is a call for a corresponding effort to explain why some citizens fail to do as well as others. Put simply, if inequality is not natural or ordained by God, how can we account for it? From the perspective of those who did not see inequality as the result of exploitation and expression, Kingsley Davis and Wilbur Moore (1944) posed the question about why inequality exists in contemporary societies to readers of the *American Sociological Review*. Their thesis would become known as the classic functionalist account of inequality. Perhaps, they suggested, inequality is inevitable because it is good for society. In their account, occupation stood in for social class, because it was seen as reflecting the impact of education on careers and the impact of occupations on income. Their argument can be summarized rather succinctly:

- Certain positions are functionally more important than others.
- There is a limited supply of individuals with the requisite skills to perform those most important positions.
- The training of talent into skill—or transforming potential into actual competence—requires sacrifices, which might be in terms of time, energy, finances, or a combination of factors.
- In order to get people to undergo the rigors required to acquire the necessary skills associated with the most important occupations, society needs to induce them to sacrifice by offering the promise of future rewards.
- The three main rewards society can offer individuals are financial gain, power, and status.
- Society benefits when the functionally most important positions are performed by skilled people.
- Therefore, inequality is not only inevitable, but is actually beneficial to society as a whole.

Davis and Moore's depiction of modern industrial societies is one in which inequality is based on individual achievement. If true, it would mean that inequality is the product of a meritocracy. While meritocratic factors shape contemporary inequality, critics of the classic functionalist argument note that it fails to consider the darker side of inequality. For example, it does not address the fact that once a system of inequality is in place, forces are set in motion that serve to perpetuate it. Self-interest and competition come into play, with those that are early "winners" having resources available to them to maintain their privileged position. It fails to consider the possibility that some types of inequality are dysfunctional (for example, wealthy leaders of drug cartels or other criminal syndicates). Nor does it consider the possibility that inequality may be the consequence of exploitation and oppression. In short, conflict theorists have called into question the underlying assumptions of Davis and Moore's functionalist theory. For our purposes, two recent concepts in theories of inequality are of particular significance: durable inequalities and intersecting inequalities.

DURABLE INEQUALITIES

Charles Tilly (1998: 6) defined durable inequalities as "those that last from one social interaction to the next," which included "those that persist over whole careers, lifetimes, and organizational histories." Unlike the individualistic focus of Davis and Moore's functionalist account, which views inequalities as arising as a result of the differing attributes of individuals, Tilly (1998: 7) argues that if inequalities prove to be durable—in other words, persisting over time—they must be constructed around categorical distinctions among people, which includes such differences as "black/white, male/female, citizen/foreigner, or Muslim/Jew rather than to individual differences in attributes, propensities, or performances."

Attempting to offer as parsimonious an explanation for durable inequalities as possible, Tilly (1998: 10) contends that there are two main causal mechanisms, which he identifies as exploitation and opportunity hoarding. Exploitation occurs when powerful people linked by social networks to one another use their power to "command resources from which they draw significantly increased returns" by controlling the efforts of the less powerful and preventing them from reaping the benefits of their efforts. Opportunity hoarding occurs when the networks of the powerful work to obtain a monopoly over the most valuable resources.

While these two mechanisms set the establishment of durable inequalities in motion, they are complemented by two additional mechanisms, emulation and adaptation, which Tilly (1998: 10) contends "cement such arrangements in place." Emulation refers to the replication of a model of inequality from one setting to another, for example from the workplace to the political system. Adaptation refers to the varied ways that inequalities are played out in everyday life, such as in selecting friendships and neighborhoods based on similar locations in the structures of categorical inequality.

Tilly's argument bears a family resemblance to Marxist accounts. For Marxists, capitalism is predicated on exploitation. Indeed, the economic system cannot exist without the capitalist class exploiting the working classes. The hegemonic class in the capitalist economy is also the ruling class in such a society's political system. His argument also parallels the thesis of Max Weber that says that once people, either individually or collectively, possess something of value, they seek to effect closure that prevents others from coming to possess it as well. This is similar to what Tilly means by opportunity hoarding.

Some critics have argued that Tilly's attempt at constructing an abstract and parsimonious theory fails to do justice to the complexity of inequality, to both the factors that create and sustain it and to the forces that serve to revise or undermine inequality (Laslett 2000). However, for our purposes in this chapter, the general idea of durable inequality based in particular on one specific categorical difference—race and ethnicity—can be a useful tool of analysis.

INTERSECTING INEQUALITIES

While the focus of this book is race and ethnicity, people are at one and the same time defined by multiple identities, with other salient aspects of identity including gender, social class, religion, sexual orientation, and disability. In recent years, scholars have become increasingly concerned about the intersecting nature of these identities. In particular, considerable attention has been devoted to the intersections of race, class, and gender. In many instances, the relationship is mutually reinforcing, though this is not necessarily always true. Thus, in the US today whites have higher average incomes than blacks and men have higher average incomes than women. If race and gender were mutually reinforcing, it would mean that black women have lower average incomes than white men, white women, and black men. And this, in fact, is the case.

In what follows, we will explore the intersecting character of inequality, focusing on the case of the US, with a brief comparison to the UK. As will become evident, this chapter is quite different from the preceding one. Whereas Chapter 2 focused on major theories accounting for prejudice and discrimination, this chapter will be highly empirical, the goal being to offer a detailed and cumulative description of contemporary patterns of racial inequality and the broader implications and consequences of those patterns.

INEQUALITY IN THE CONTEMPORARY UNITED STATES

The fact that the United States is the advanced industrial nation with the highest level of inequality in the world is virtually undisputed by scholars today. There are a variety of ways that social scientists attempt to understand the extent and the scope of inequality.

INCOME INEQUALITY

One of the most commonly used measuring sticks is income distribution. Employing this measure, we find a highly skewed distribution pattern. In 2009, the bottom fifth of all households with the lowest incomes received only 3.4 percent of the total income earned that year, while the second quintile earned 8.6 percent, the middle quintile 14.6 percent, the next to the top quintile 23.2 percent, and the top quintile earned 50.3 percent. In other words, the top 20 percent of the population possessed slightly over half of all earned income. The top 5 percent of the population—or in other words, those at the top of the highest quintile—earned 21.7 percent of the total. These distribution figures are the most recent in a significant trend that began in the 1970s. During the past thirty years, beginning in 1974, the percentages earned by the lowest quintile fell 2.1 percent, the second quintile lost 3.3 percent, and the third quintile lost 2.7 percent. The fourth quintile has shown small up and down fluctuations, currently down 0.6 percent, and the percent of total income of the top quintile has increased 8.8 percent (US Census Bureau 2009; Jones and Weinberg 2000: 4).

A similar trend is demonstrated by evaluating income inequality over time. During the 1980s, the entire income structure expanded dramatically, with the top stretching upward away from the center and the center moving up away from the bottom. In the 1990s, the gap between the ninetieth and fiftieth percentile continued to grow, increasing inequality between the top tenth and the rest of the population, while at the same time the difference between the fiftieth and tenth percentiles shrank. Since 1999, however, it appears that the decreasing inequality in the bottom half of the income structure has stopped, and has shown signs of increasing while the widening disparity between the top and the middle persists (Mishel, *et al.* 2003: 152). In fact, the highest incomes have continuously increased at rather rapid rates. In 1979, about 13,500 US taxpayers claimed incomes equivalent to $1 million or more. By 1994, the number earning this much had exceeded 68,000. The disparities between the salaries of executives and their employees have widened considerably as CEO and other executive-level salaries have soared, particularly so since the 1990s. The increased use of stock options as a key component of many executive pay packages has led to much higher levels of income inequality. In 1965, the average CEO earned 24 times more than the average worker. Thirty years later, in 1995, that figure had soared to 100 times the average worker's income. By 2005, the figure hit 262 (Mishel 2006; see also Hacker and Pierson 2010).

Robert Frank and Philip Cook (1995) have explored the runaway incomes at the top of the distribution, which are fed by "winner-take-all" markets. The most popular musicians, athletes, actors, artists, authors, car manufacturers, and even producers of food and ordinary household items increasingly tend to receive a disproportionate amount of the monetary benefits in their respective markets, pushing those of only slightly lesser quality (and sometimes of equal quality) far down the income scale, if not out of the market entirely. Indeed, the mean income of the top 5 percent of earners in the United States nearly doubled in a decade, from $138,000 in 1991 to $260,000 in 2001, while earners further down the distribution ladder made comparatively meager gains (US Census Bureau 2003, all dollar figures adjusted for parity).

WEALTH INEQUALITY

However, while the income and wage distributions do provide a glimpse of the extent of inequality in the US, a factor that even more profoundly gets at the heart of inequality is wealth. Wealth, determined by a household's assets minus debts, is distributed even more unevenly than income. Wealth is an especially important consideration shaping economic security in changing times. The wealthiest people in the society have in their wealth a buffer from downward economic trends and family and other crises that is not always available to the middle class and when it is it is far more limited, while being largely absent from the working class and the poor. If a household experiences financial hardship—the loss of a job, illness, and so forth—wealth is the cushion that breaks a fall. Given this reality, a significant portion of the US population lives in very vulnerable circumstances. Only one-third of households has any (or has negative) financial assets, and the average family in 1988 held $3,700 in net financial assets, enough to sustain them at the poverty line for a mere three months (Oliver and Shapiro 1997: 69). The economic precariousness of the entire bottom half of the population is in stark contrast to their more affluent counterparts. In 1992, the wealthiest quintile possessed a whopping 84 percent of the wealth in the US, and was the beneficiary of 99 percent of the wealth gain between 1983 and 1989. The bottom 80 percent of households received a mere 1 percent of the increase (Marshall 2000: 5). By 2007, the top quintile of households owned 93 percent of nation's financial wealth. This meant that 80 percent of the population owned only 7 percent of the total financial wealth. As further indication of the highly skewed character of wealth inequality, the top 1 percent of households own 43 percent of financial wealth (Domhoff 2011).

CLASS, RACE, AND GENDER

Much of this social class inequality tracks along lines defined by race and gender. First, considering the racial data depicted in Figure 3.1, in 2009 the median income for Asian households was about $65,500, $54,500 for non-Hispanic white households, $38,000 for Hispanic households, and $32,000 for African American households. These annual incomes are complemented by Figure 3.2, which looks at differences in weekly earnings of full-time workers by race.

Whereas only 9.4 percent of non-Hispanic whites were living at or below the poverty line in 2010, 12.2 percent of Asians, 25.3 percent of Hispanics, 26.4 percent of American Indians and Alaska Natives, and 25.8 percent of blacks lived in poverty. Even when they are found in the same occupations and work full-time and year-round, Asian men earn 94 percent of the income of white men, Hispanic men only 86 percent, and black men only 84 percent (Weller 2010).

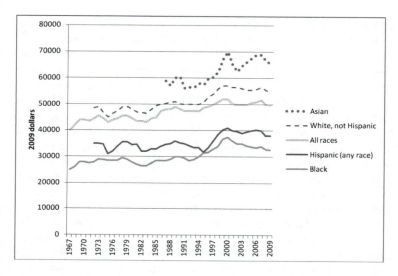

Figure 3.1: Real median household income by race and Hispanic origin, 1967 to 2009.

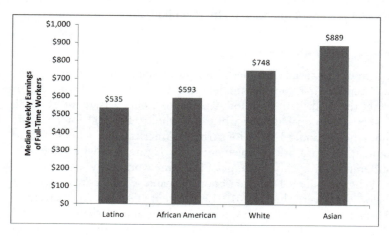

Figure 3.2: The racial gap in earning, 2008.

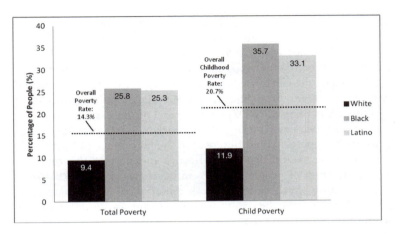

Figure 3.3: Poverty rate by race, 2010 (source: Weller 2010).

Wealth is similarly divided along racial lines. While a quarter of white households possess no wealth or negative wealth, 61 percent of black and 54 percent of Hispanic households fit into this category. While 38 percent of white households lack the financial assets to survive for three months at the poverty line, as many as 73 percent of Hispanic households and 80 percent of black households live in this precarious financial position (Oliver and Shapiro 1997: 86–87). Viewed another way, the median white household possesses $7,000 in net financial assets, in contrast to the zero assets held by the median black household. The median white household has over eight times the net worth of the median black household (Mishel, *et al.* 2003: 284).

Even considering only middle class households, whether it is defined by income ($25,000 to $50,000, calculated with 1988 dollars), college education, or white-collar occupation, black households possess only 35 percent of the net worth of white households in the first definition, 23 percent by the second, and 15 percent by the third. In terms of financial assets—that which can help prevent financial disaster in extenuating circumstances—black households have between 1 and 4 percent that of whites, with white-collar black households having no net financial assets whatsoever, a figure that excludes equity in a home or vehicle (Oliver and Shapiro 1997: 94).

This means that the average black middle class family has to rely almost entirely on income alone for its middle class standard of living, and cannot withstand a single financial obstacle without it becoming a potential financial catastrophe. Figure 3.4 uses data from 2007 to depict the gap in wealth based on race for whites, Latinos, and African Americans, providing an update to the pioneering work done by Oliver and Shapiro (1997) near the end of the past century. This figure is complemented by Figure 3.5, which indicates racial disparities in assets by reporting on differences in the percentage of households that are asset poor. This is, in effect, a measure of the common characterization of people living from paycheck to paycheck. While not quite from paycheck to paycheck, a household is defined as asset poor if does not have the wealth resources to subsist for three months without income during that period.

The disparity in earnings by gender has significantly decreased in recent decades; however, the gap between women and men remains and it is not an insignificant gap. In 1984, full-time, year-round working women of privileged racial groups—white and Asian—made 68–77 percent that of white men *in the same occupations*; men of the least privileged racial groups—Hispanic and black—earned 84 to 86 percent that of white men. However, since 1984, women of all races combined (irrespective of occupation) have jumped from an average

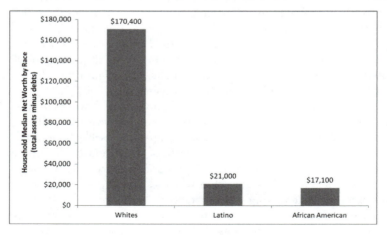

Figure 3.4: The racial wealth gap, 2007 (source: Federal Reserve, 2007 Survey of Consumer Finances Public Data Set).

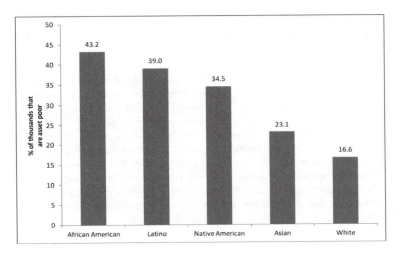

Figure 3.5: Asset poverty by race, 2004 (source: Corporation for Enterprise Development, 2007–2008 Assets and Opportunity Scorecard, analysis base).
Data note: A household is asset poor if it has insufficient net wealth to subsist at the federal poverty level for three months in the absence of income.

$0.64 per men's dollar to $0.76 per men's dollar. Whereas men's incomes have made little progress since 1973 (then $27,802, and $29,101 in 2001), women's incomes have increased 72 percent—up from $9,649 in 1973 to $16,614 in 2001 (US Census Bureau 2001). This can be construed as welcome change in the right direction. However, substantial inequalities still exist for women. Box 3.1 depicts the impact of the intersection of race and gender as a young black woman describes the precariousness of her employment situation.

Box 3.1: Roberta: everyday life for the working poor.

Roberta, a mother of two young children, graduated from high school before she had her kids. She had an entry-level clerical job with United Parcel Service and had hoped to move up the managerial ladder in that firm. Her lack of white-collar experience and limited skills made that unlikely, so she left UPS and found a job at Burger Barn, where she was soon advanced to the position of a salaried manager. Roberta earned almost $400 a week as a manager, a yearly gross income of about $19,000.

She could make ends meet on that salary as long as nothing went wrong. Roberta's retired parents were able to take care of her youngest child during her work hours and ferried her older son to and from school, which relieved her of the need to pay for child care. She was living in a public housing project near her parents' home, and was fortunate to have a two-bedroom apartment for a modest rent. As long as everyone in her family was in good health, Roberta was okay. Unexpected illnesses presented major problems [as she explains], "You have no medical benefits [in my job]. If my kids get chicken pox, I have to take them to the hospital. I have to pay out of my pocket. [Burger Barn] is not paying me that great, you know."

Source: Newman 1999: 152

Comparisons of racial inequalities between the US and the UK are made somewhat more complicated because of differences in types and levels of data collection. That being said, Britain's racial minorities are generally defined as blacks, South Asians, and others (including the Chinese). Blacks can be further subdivided in the Caribbeans, Africans, and others, while South Asians can be divided into Indians, Pakistanis, and Bangladeshis. These are all immigrant groups, the vast majority of which arrived in the UK from the middle of the past century forward, beginning in the post-World War II era when the nation confronted labor shortages and in some instances actively recruited immigrants from former colonies. The vast majority of these immigrants, in fact, came from Commonwealth nations.

Whites have higher average incomes than people of color, but the differences vary depending on the group. The Indian community has the highest average incomes, while the Bangladeshi has the lowest—and not surprisingly, the latter has the highest rates of poverty and the lowest rates of labor force participation (Mason 2000: 43–63). Evidence points to the persistence of discrimination in hiring, but policies aimed at combating discrimination have had some impact in improving opportunities. In terms of the poverty rate, the rate for Indians is comparable to that of whites, while it is twice as high for Black Africans, higher still for Pakistanis, and the highest for Bangladeshis. Related to this, the unemployment rates of the poorest groups is much higher than the white population: for Pakistanis it is twice as high, while for Bangladeshis it is three time higher (Pilkington 2003).

THE CONSEQUENCES OF INEQUALITY: CONSTRAINTS ON EQUAL OPPORTUNITY

What are the implications of these existing levels of inequality on life chances? This is the topic we turn to in the following section. While a vast majority of Americans claim to embrace the idea of equal opportunity (but not equality of outcomes), the issue becomes one of sorting out the various ways that existing levels of inequality impede the realization of creating an equal opportunity society. In this section, we will explore the following issues: (1) quality of life issues associated with physical and mental health; (2) food and nutrition; (3) housing and neighborhood quality; (4) crime; (5) environmental risk; (6) schooling and the development of **human capital**; and (7) **social capital**.

It should be stressed at the outset that this is only a snapshot of aspects of the consequences of inequality. What is clear is that inequality is a complex and multidimensional phenomenon. What follows is by no means intended to be comprehensive. Rather, its purpose is to illustrate some of the key multifaceted elements involved in determining the varied impacts of inequality on different sectors of the disadvantaged population.

QUALITY OF LIFE ISSUES: PHYSICAL AND MENTAL HEALTH

Inequality in the United States is in no way limited simply to economics. The "losers" in this unequal society endure a number of consequences deriving from their lower socioeconomic status, consequences that pervade virtually all aspects of life. One of these is a generic term called "quality of life." While this term can be used to account for a number of factors, we concentrate here on only two: mental and physical health.

To begin with, numerous studies have demonstrated that low socioeconomic status is correlated with a wide range of psychological disorders. Although the direction of causality is still debated, Mary Merva and Richard Fowles' (2000) study of the mental health of laid-off workers suggests that financial privation, at least in some cases, precedes psychiatric distress. Furthermore, it appears that not only is *absolute* economic deprivation strongly associated with mental health, but so too is *relative* deprivation. Increasing inequality causes those in the lower rungs of the wage scale to feel alienated from the rest of society and to increasingly view themselves as inadequate.

Mental health problems frequently result from the negative impacts of poverty and inequality, and once individuals are suffering from a mental illness, they become less likely to find or keep gainful employment. Add to this the fact that the mentally ill are often left untreated, particularly if they do not have insurance to pay for counseling or medication. More of the poor with treatable mental illnesses go untreated than is the case with the general population.

Pressure to "keep up with the Joneses" is strong throughout the society, but for those at the bottom it is especially stressful because success seems to be out of reach. Indeed, the lower class is no less influenced than the middle class by the values of a consumer culture, despite the fact that there are so many goods and services that they cannot possibly afford to purchase. Michael Hughes and Melvin Thomas (1998) demonstrate that African Americans experience a lower quality of life (measurements include life satisfaction, marital happiness, mistrust, happiness, anomie, and health) than whites, even when classified as middle or upper class. The authors suggest that this is due to a "racial tax"—the harmful psychological effects of a long historical legacy of racism.

The physical health consequences of inequality are no less serious. Regardless of the exact measurement used, low-income level and poor health are strongly linked. For example, impoverished African Americans endure disproportionately high incidences of high blood pressure, heart problems, diabetes and its complications, and sudden infant death syndrome. Cancer (among males), sickle-cell anemia, tuberculosis, hypertension, arteriosclerosis, and AIDS also affect significantly higher percentages of blacks than whites. Because of the high concentration of blacks among the poor, it is likely that these are related to poverty and not only to racism. Life expectancy is another factor that varies considerably by race, gender, socioeconomic status

(SES), and also location. Arline Geronimus and colleagues (2001) found that the life expectancy at age 16 of a black man living in urban poverty is 42 years.

This may be in part due to the fact that those in poverty tend to exhibit more unhealthy behaviors than the rest of the population. Smoking, in particular, appears to be concentrated among those of low SES and among racial minorities. The disparity in health is also in large part due to an under-use of health care. One-third of the African-American deaths above the white death rate are the result of treatable conditions. Much of this is certainly due to the fact that access to health care is severely limited for low socioeconomic status Americans, and the number of people without health insurance has recently increased. In 2003, 15.6 percent of the population was without coverage, amounting to 45 million people, 1.4 million more than in 2002. Employer-provided health insurance is decreasing as health care costs increase, and those who still have insurance via an employer are expected to pay larger portions of the premiums even as quality of care is decreasing due to the increasing adoption of managed care plans. These recent trends most sharply affect the lower classes—as income level decreases, so does access to quality health insurance—and racial minorities, particularly Hispanics, of whom nearly a third have no health coverage (DeNavas-Walt, *et al.* 2004: 14–15). The Patient Protection and Affordable Care Act, signed into law by President Barack Obama in 2010, is intended to expand health insurance coverage to a sizeable percentage of the previously uninsured. At this writing, the legislation is being introduced incrementally, while simultaneously confronting various legislative and judicial challenges. If the law survives the challenges, it has the potential for addressing some of the most glaring disparities in health care coverage.

Living in hazardous neighborhoods and being exposed to injurious work conditions further endangers the physical health of the disadvantaged. Individuals at the bottom of the social structure are more likely to hold jobs that involve heavy lifting, awkward body postures, exposure to toxic substances, dust, fumes, explosives, acids, and other harmful substances as well as long hours of mechanical, routinized actions. These hazards are also correlated with race. All of these take a toll on the bodies and on the life expectancies of the most disadvantaged sectors of the society.

FOOD AND NUTRITION

Food insufficiency is another problem that disproportionately affects racial minorities, low-income households, and female-headed households. Katherine Alaimo and colleagues (1998) estimate that 4.1 percent of the overall US population—between 9–12 million people—does not have enough food to eat either occasionally or frequently. However, in their study of Minneapolis-St. Paul, 15.2 percent of Mexican Americans fell into this category; even when controlling for other economic and demographic factors, twice as many Mexican Americans as whites claimed to experience food deficiency. Nearly 8 percent of African Americans reported food deficiency compared to 2.5 percent of non-Hispanic whites, which at least in part is attributable to disparities in SES. Obviously, SES plays an enormous role in food sufficiency; 14 percent of the low-income population does not have enough food at times. Other studies report even higher percentages of hunger levels. Forty-five percent of children living under the poverty line in 2002 suffered food insecurity. America's Second Harvest, the nation's largest food relief distributor, came to the assistance of 23.3 million people in 2001; the median income for those helped was well below the poverty line (Rank 2004: 38). Getting enough food to eat can be especially problematic for the poor during the winter months. Jayanta Bhattacharya and research associates (2002) found that while both the rich and poor increase heating expenditures in very cold times, the poor compensate for this increase by reducing their food expenditures by about the same cost. While the rich tend to increase their food intake, the poor eat about 200 fewer calories than in warmer months. This "heat or eat" dilemma significantly impacts the nutrition and the health of the poor.

Making matters worse, Chanjin Chung and Samuel Myers (1999) demonstrate that food actually costs more for the urban poor. They found a $16.62 difference in market-basket prices, or the cost for a week's worth of food that meets minimum nutritional requirements, between chain and non-chain grocery stores. Because many chain stores are not located in or near urban poor neighborhoods, and many poor people do not have cars or adequate public transportation, residents have little choice but to shop at closer, but more expensive non-chain stores. Furthermore, these non-chain stores carry a far smaller selection of certain types of foods, particularly fresh produce, meat, and dairy products.

Inequality does not only impact food in terms of insufficiency and hunger. Many people conceive of eating disorders as being primarily white, middle- to upper-class female phenomena, resulting from social pressures to conform to our culture's thin ideal of beauty. However, these disorders have class, race, and sexual orientation dimensions as well. Some women develop bulimia, anorexia, unhealthy dieting, and bingeing as a means of coping with such "traumas" as discrimination and high levels of stress based on the factors just mentioned. For example, many women living in poverty respond to the stress of their lives by using food as a drug. Excessive eating can produce effects similar to alcohol consumption, is far cheaper, and does not result in hangovers that would hinder productivity. This can explain one of the unusual features of contemporary poverty. While there is hunger, it is also true that poor people are more likely to be overweight than the general population. Obesity and its related problems, such as hypertension and diabetes, result not only from overeating, but from eating cheaper but unhealthy foods, particularly those high in saturated fat.

HOUSING AND NEIGHBORHOOD QUALITY

Inequality also profoundly affects housing and neighborhood quality. Housing discrimination based primarily on race remains an endemic problem in the United States, which, combined with a shortage of decent affordable housing, is responsible for the concentration of poverty in select geographic areas. While some of the most overt forms of housing discrimination are far less obvious since the civil rights era, new and more subtle modes of discrimination persist, many of them difficult to detect. For example, John Yinger (1986) has demonstrated that housing agents show blacks 36 percent fewer apartments than they show whites; more to the point, they purposefully do not introduce them to apartments located in predominantly white neighborhoods. To make matters worse, even when SES is controlled, blacks looking to procure housing in black neighborhoods are significantly less likely to be approved for a loan than are their white counterparts. This is in part due to **redlining** practices and in part due to discriminatory lending policies. And when blacks do move into predominantly white areas, they often must endure the antagonisms directed at them by white residents. Whites searching for new homes will tend to avoid the neighborhood, and as a result, minority households will eventually dominate it. The above is true for Hispanics as well, though to a lesser extent.

Box 3.2: Discrimination in housing markets.

Douglas Massey has studied the impact of segregation on life chances over several decades and has concluded that residential segregation continues to be a particularly intractable reality in contemporary American life, as the following passage reveals:

Racial discrimination in markets for goods, services, and employment was only banned in 1964; in real estate and insurance markets in 1968, and in lending markets in 1974. Since the close of the Civil Rights Era, access and treatment has improved for African Americans in many markets, with especially large gains in those for goods and services but with significant improvement also in markets for labor, credit, and finance. But in one market progress has been exceedingly slow, almost glacial: that for housing. High levels of discrimination in real estate and high levels of housing segregation are ongoing realities.

Source: Massey 2006: 127

What is the result of this geographic segregation? Douglas Massey and Eric Fong (1990) show that while highly educated black communities can truly uphold a "separate but equal" status with socioeconomically similar white communities, poorer and less educated blacks experience neighborhood conditions inferior to other impoverished populations due to their relative concentration in urban inner city settings. These are neighborhoods characterized by what Massey and Nancy Denton (1993) call "**hypersegregation**." Police protection, firefighting, sanitation services, and similar municipal services tend to be of poorer quality in low SES areas, and children have fewer places to play, and an even smaller numbers of *safe* recreation areas. More youth in these neighborhoods drop out of high school, have decreased childhood IQ, and become pregnant as teenagers. Those who live in impoverished and racially segregated (especially African American, but to a lesser degree Mexican American) neighborhoods suffer significantly higher mortality rates, even when variance in individual characteristics is controlled. In terms of employment prospects, hypersegregated neighborhoods have become "jobless ghettoes" that are plagued by crime, prostitution, drug trafficking, and gang activity. Often, potential employers do not welcome individuals raised in these locales, in part due to discrimination, but also in part due to the underdevelopment of skills in these communities; unfortunately, this inability to find work only reinforces and thus perpetuates disadvantage.

Box 3.3: Jobless neighborhoods.

William Julius Wilson has studied the decline in job opportunities in inner-cities. In this passage from his book, *When Work Disappears*, he describes what many inner-city residents think about the way potential employers treat them:

> Many inner city residents have a strong sense of the negative attitudes which employers tend to have toward them. A 33-year old employed janitor from a poor South Side [of Chicago] neighborhood had this observation: "I went to a coupla jobs where a couple of the receptionists told me in confidence: 'You know what they do with applications from blacks as soon as the day is over?' Say 'we rip them and throw 'em in the garbage.'" In addition to concerns about being rejected because of race, the fears that some inner-city residents have of being denied employment simply because of their inner-city address or neighborhood are not unfounded. A welfare mother who lives in a large public housing project put it this way: "Honestly, I believe they look at the address and the—your attitudes, your address, your surround—you know, your environment has a lot to do with your employment status. The people with the best addresses have the best chances, I feel so, I feel so."
>
> Source: Wilson 1996: 137

CRIME AND PUNISHMENT

Socioeconomic and racial inequality also negatively affects crime and violence. In terms of racial inequality, in 2002 49 percent of all murder victims were black, 49 percent were white, while only 13 percent of Americans are black and 80 percent are white. Blacks are seven times more likely than whites to commit murder, and six times more likely to be murdered. Turning to another type of crime, households earning less than $7,500 were victims of burglary and assault at significantly higher rates than higher earning households (Bureau of Justice Statistics 2003). Why blacks and those of low SES are so much more likely to be exposed to crime is the object of much speculation. Of interest to this discussion, there is empirical evidence indicating that for whites, low socioeconomic status is strongly correlated with violent crime. For blacks, on the other hand, this is not the case.

A possible explanation for this is put forward by Richard Alba, John Logan, and Paul Bellair (1994). In their study, which focused on suburbs, they also found that black SES, and additionally family structure and other personal traits, do not explain the race's disproportionately large exposure to crime. Rather than these factors, they suggest that the culprit is the residential segregation process that locates blacks—even if affluent—in crime-prone areas. Neighborhoods characterized by a high percentage of disadvantaged households (including high levels of lower class families, minority households, and female-headed households), immigrants, and residential instability are less likely to have strong ties to one another and to uphold informal social control, such as watching over neighbors' property, keeping track of neighbors' kids, and so forth. Thus, they experience much higher rates of crime and violence because they lack the control necessary to prevent these things from happening.

In general, insofar as high levels of inequality are associated with high crime levels and socioeconomic inequality and racial inequality are intertwined, it is not surprising that disadvantaged racial minorities are involved in crime at a great rate than the general population, both as offenders and victims. There is evidence to suggest that this is particularly the case in instances of violent crime.

The significance of class location and racial identity is reflected in the state's punishment practices for criminal violations. The United

States imprisons far more of its citizens per capita than any other advanced industrial nation. It incarcerates approximately 600 individuals per 100,000. The average for other advanced industrial nations ranges from around 55 to 120 per 100,000. The rate in Scandinavian countries, for example, is one-tenth the US rate. Moreover, the US sends people to prison for much longer periods of time than is the case in other economically comparable nations. The typical prisoner in both state and federal prisons is relatively young and relatively poor. It is also the case that blacks disproportionately constitute the largest plurality of the current prison population. At present, the United States imprisons almost 1.5 million individuals, 44 percent of which were black, compared to 35 percent white, 19 percent Latino, and 2 percent other (Human Rights Watch 2002).

A similar scenario can be seen in the use of the death penalty—a practice that has been abolished in virtually all other advanced industrial nations. Mark Costanzo (1997: 84) summarizes the nature of the racial disparities in capital punishment cases in the following way:

> Those who are accused of murdering a white victim are more likely to be charged with a capital crime; those convicted of killing a white victim are more likely to receive a death sentence; black defendants who are convicted of killing a white person are the group most likely to receive the death penalty; [and] white defendants who murder black victims are the group least likely to receive a death sentence.

While 58 percent of the defendants executed between 1976 and 2004 were white, at 34 percent, blacks are overrepresented. Moreover, as of 2004, blacks and whites had nearly reached parity in terms of their respective percentages of the death row population, with blacks registering at 42 percent and whites at 46 percent (NAACP Legal Defense Fund 2004).

The capacity of the state to punish its citizenry is a reflection of its monopoly on the power to do so. The need to punish large numbers of citizens is related to levels of inequality. It is not fortuitous that the United States has the highest level of inequality among the advanced industrial nations and it also has, by far, the highest level of incarceration along with being the only one routinely using the death penalty. Social control, in short, is more problematic and difficult to achieve in highly unequal societies.

ENVIRONMENTAL RISK

Those at the bottom of the social class system and the racial hierarchy are not only endangered by greater violence and crime, but also by environmental hazards. Because minimizing pollution and toxic wastes is costly, plants that produce these byproducts tend to carefully locate themselves in areas where land is less expensive, where residents are not likely to protest their presence, and where challenges to their mishandling of wastes is least likely. These locations are found in low SES and minority communities. In the Southeast, 26 percent to 42 percent of households proximal to (within the same census tract as) a hazardous waste landfill live in poverty. Other sources of environmental dangers plague the disadvantaged as well. As many as 68 percent of urban African American children living in households earning less than $6,000 yearly suffer dangerous levels of lead in their blood. On the other hand, white children in families above $15,000 experience unsafe lead levels at a rate of only 12 percent. Likewise, impoverished children are nearly 40 percent more likely to be exposed to cigarette smoke in the home than those above the poverty line. Air pollution (carbon monoxide and nitrogen dioxide) from stoves and heating systems is also far more prevalent in low-income homes. Water pollution affects primarily rural, low SES populations, including poor Mexican Americans residing near the nation's southern border. As noted earlier, a variety of environmental risks are associated with various low-income occupations (Evans and Kantrowitz 2002).

While these and related environmental risks have profound effects on their victims' health, often due to daily exposure year after year, other less apparent environmental factors also deeply influence the lives of the urban poor. First, exposure to high levels of noise pollution is also linked with low SES. Not only does constant clamor often result in hearing damage, but also it has been shown to elevate stress, to impede the execution of complex tasks, to hinder children's mastery of reading, and to undermine the development of certain crucial "interpersonal processes" related to the emergence of altruism and the control of aggression. Furthermore, it may also spur feelings of helplessness and inhibit motivation—apparently from the individual's inability to control the noise.

Overcrowding (less than one room per resident) is yet another environmental risk factor associated with SES. Living in crowded conditions has virtually the same results as noise exposure and also contributes to the spread of infectious diseases. Overcrowding is not limited to the home. This also translates to outdoor space, both in the yard as well as in park areas: children in low-income New York City neighborhoods average about 17 square yards of park space per child, whereas the rest of the city's children each have 40 square yards (Evans and Kantrowitz 2002).

While there are many environmental risks, such as air pollution, that are shared by all sectors of the population, it is clearly the case that environmental risks in general disproportionately impact lower income people and disadvantaged racial minorities.

SCHOOLING AND THE DEVELOPMENT OF HUMAN CAPITAL

Race and social class inequality, more than gender inequality, result in vast educational disadvantages for lower class and minority children. These inequities appear to be rooted in three main factors: unequal funding for schools; family structure and parental involvement in their child's education; and discrimination. First, school funding is based largely on local property taxes. This means that schools located in areas populated primarily with lower class households are going to have significantly smaller budgets than schools in wealthier middle to upper class districts. However, this inequality is exacerbated in the inner cities, where lower class youth and racial minorities are likely to be concentrated. Operating inner city schools tends to be more expensive than running suburban schools. The school properties themselves tend to cost more, and the upkeep and insurance of the buildings, which are often old and subject to frequent vandalism, demands a larger portion of the educational budget than elsewhere. Furthermore, other needs of inner cities, such as large police forces and fire departments, compete with the neighborhood schools for limited local tax revenues.

Despite *Brown v. Board of Education of Topeka*, the 1954 landmark Supreme Court decision that found that segregated schools led to racially unequal educational opportunities, a half century after the decision, American schools are undergoing a process of resegregation. In a study conducted by Harvard's Civil Rights Project, the researchers have determined that the gains made in the 1960s and 1970s have eroded and particularly in the 1990s, the rate of resegregation has increased dramatically. At present, 70 percent of black students attend schools that contain predominantly minority student populations, while Latinos have, too, witnessed increasing levels of educational segregation (Street 2005). Thus minority students, particularly poorer ones, increasingly attend public schools that are inferior to those of their white counterparts.

In general, less money is spent per capita on the education of low SES and minority youth than on higher social class whites. Somewhat more debated is the effect of this on disadvantaged students. The frequently cited Coleman Report, which appeared in 1966, convinced many that school characteristics, most of which can be linked directly to the school's economic resources, have very little bearing on student achievement. The report argued that the single most important factor was the role played by parents. However, more recent research has contradicted this finding. School resources and class size both appear to affect students' test scores, and going to underprivileged schools has been demonstrated to be as strong a predictor of low future SES as intelligence. It is not surprising that youth who attend schools that utilize dated textbooks and have inadequate or no science labs, inadequate library materials, underpaid teachers, large classrooms, and a lack of access to computer technologies are at a significant disadvantage compared to those who attend schools with well-paid instructors, are provided individualized attention, and have access to up-to-date educational materials.

Coleman was not entirely wrong since family characteristics and parental involvement do affect education by race and SES as well. Vincent Roscigno and James Ainsworth-Darnell (1999) have shown that high SES parents tend to provide their children with more household educational resources (periodicals, reference materials, computers, books, calculators), enroll their children in more non-school classes involving art, music, or dance, and take their children on more cultural trips to museums, historical sites, concerts, and so forth. Interestingly, while white students who receive these household benefits appear to benefit from them (as measured by higher grades and test scores), black students do not receive the same educational return.

Parental interaction with their children also facilitates educational success. Hence, children in single-parent households tend to operate at an educational disadvantage; single parents supervise their children's homework less often and generally have less contact with their children. Research provides evidence that a high level of parental involvement in a school boosts student achievement. However, since single working parents generally have little time available to attend PTA meetings and other such activities, their students do not receive this benefit to their education to the same extent as more privileged students in two-family households. Moreover, female-headed households are disproportionately characteristic of minority families and lower class families, reflecting the interactive impact of race, class, and gender (Pong 1998).

Finally, simple discrimination appears to explain much of the leftover disparity in educational achievement between blacks and whites. The racial difference in academic success is profound. African Americans on average are as many as four years behind white students in reading, math, science, and writing. They are more likely to be held back a grade. They are less likely to attend and complete college. They are vastly underrepresented at the top of national test distributions. Although black students at higher SES schools score higher on the SAT than do those at lower SES schools, they do not perform as well as their white classmates. While many of these differences can be explained by the aforementioned economic and family factors, these do not fully account for the differences. Although discrimination is far less easy to operationalize, it seems highly likely that racial discrimination also plays a part in educational inequality.

Although women do not experience significant educational differences from men before graduating from high school, there are gender disparities in higher education. In many ways, of the many inequalities discussed in this chapter, this may be the arena in which women and men are nearly equal, with women sometimes even surpassing men. A slightly higher percentage of women (among whites and in virtually all minority groups) enroll in college and graduate with two-year, bachelors, masters, and professional degrees compared to men. However, only 37.3 percent of PhD degrees were earned by women in 1992, and they remain a minority among college and university faculty. Additionally, women tend to be disproportionately enrolled in less selective schools; men still enroll in and receive degrees from choice institutions at higher rates than women (Jacobs 1996).

Many of these factors related to higher education provide evidence for the perpetuation of racial disparities. A smaller percentage of African Americans and Hispanics enroll in colleges and universities than do whites; in 2000, 39 percent of eighteen- to twenty-four-year-old whites were enrolled, 31 percent of blacks, and 22 percent of Hispanics. Additionally, the percentage of degrees earned by blacks decreases as the level of the degree increases, earning 11 percent of associate's degrees, 9 percent of bachelor's, 8 percent of master's, 7 percent of professional, and 5 percent of doctorate degrees. For Hispanics, the respective percentages are 9 percent, 6 percent, 4 percent, 5 percent, and 3 percent (Hoffman, *et al.* 2003: 93–97).

Education has a direct effect on the development of human capital, or one's skill, education, and experience that can be used to secure a quality position or to advance in the job market. As mentioned above, lower class students and racial minorities do not receive educations equivalent to their more advantaged counterparts, and therefore are often at a human capital disadvantage that starts early in childhood. Insofar as the school system in the nation fails to provide genuinely equal educational opportunities, it serves to reinforce existing inequalities rather than contributing to overcoming them.

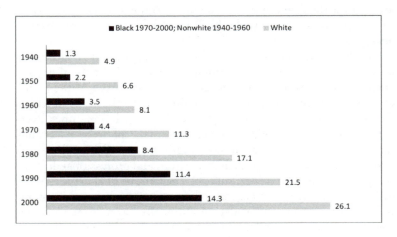

Figure 3.6: Percentage of the population twenty-five years and over with a bachelor's degree or more, by race, in the US.

SOCIAL CAPITAL

Inequality not only leads to vast discrepancies in social capital, but also perpetuates it by deterring upward mobility for those at the bottom of the social structure and by facilitating it for those already near the top. Nan Lin (2000: 786) describes social capital as "the quantity and/or quality of resources that an actor (be it an individual or group or community) can access or use through its location in a social network." Access to these resources, then, enables people to attain higher paying and more prestigious jobs as well as other quality of life benefits.

While social capital is important to the attainment of socioeconomic status, its benefits are distributed highly inequitably by initial SES location, gender, and race. Since individuals tend to maintain social networks with others of similar characteristics, the networks of members of the lower class tend to consist primarily of other low SES contacts. These connections tend not only to be lacking in the number of beneficial resources for socioeconomic advancement, but also lack the diversity of resources that are available to those of higher SES. In his review of the literature, Alejandro Portes (1998) explains that all too frequently for inner city residents, social networks do not reach outside of the inner city, and therefore, their knowledge of and ability to obtain good jobs is severely limited. Furthermore, since inner city communities tend to be more transitory, even the social ties within these poor locales are likely to be less extensive and more tenuous as a result.

Clearly, these factors have implications for race as well. African Americans have less extensive networks than Hispanics and whites, with whites having the largest networks. Since blacks are often segregated in certain neighborhoods, their social networks consist largely of other African Americans, which is not advantageous in an economy more or less dominated by whites. Even in the middle and upper classes, blacks often have relatively few weak ties to white networks, instead forming strong social ties among themselves (Lin 2000). These differences play out in explicit ways, for example, when a person seeking a job begins to turn to people they know who might assist them. Blacks tend not to have the social capital that will work to their advantage. But social capital also works in more implicit ways, as well. The example of IQ scores, which are the product of the social forces that shape one's background, is revealing. Black children adopted by white families tend to demonstrate higher IQ scores than those adopted by black families, but black children adopted by black families that have ties to racially diverse networks or predominantly white networks have higher IQs than those in black families that do not have these social network characteristics. It appears that disparities in social capital between blacks and whites contribute to the lower socioeconomic attainment of blacks.

CONCLUSION

This chapter reveals that the US is far from a nation that can be defined as offering its citizens equal opportunity for economic success. Given that blacks and Native Americans (the data contained herein for the latter is somewhat more limited) have been in the country since before its founding, and since they continue to lag behind whites and others in the society, they offer vivid testimony of the continuing impact of what Tilly has called durable inequality. Income disparities persist, while the huge disparities in wealth distribution reveal the economic precariousness of most racial minorities. Moreover, as a substantial section of the chapter documents, income and wealth inequalities have profound implications for all facets of people's lives, from where they live and go to school to what sorts of jobs they are likely to have, to their health and well-being.

4

ETHNIC CONFLICT

Conflict is a feature of any social setting in which two or more parties have differing and competing interests, and given the pervasiveness of conflict it is unsurprising that sociologists have paid considerable attention to the phenomenon, including developing a number of general theories of conflict. Conflict was central to the work of Karl Marx, who is generally seen today as one of the foundational figures of the discipline despite the fact that he never claimed to be a sociologist. In Marxist theory, one type of conflict was defined as of far more consequence than all other types of conflict: class conflict. Max Weber, a non-Marxist who was nonetheless influenced by Marx, offered a more generalized perspective on conflict, but he, too, placed particular emphasis on class-based conflict and on the significance of differences of power between competing parties in conflictual situations. Perhaps the theorist most responsible for developing a broader, more inclusive view of conflict—one that placed class conflict alongside many other forms of conflict—is Randall Collins (1975).

Summarizing the state of conflict theory today, Stephen K. Sanderson (2007: 662) contends that conflict theories, despite their differences, share four basic presuppositions, which we summarize below:

- Conflict, which can be between individuals or collectivities, arises as a consequence of opposing interests (which can be material or ideal) or of competing for scarce resources. For example, conflict can occur over formulas for school funding. Funding based on local property taxes favors privileged communities with better tax bases at the expense of poorer communities, while formulas based on state or federal funding can enhance funding to poorer communities by redistributing resources in order to promote equality in educational opportunities. Not surprisingly, conflict over competing ways to finance public education often pits wealthy suburban communities against both residents of inner cities and poor rural communities.

- Conflict can occur over many types of interests and resources. Individuals can and sometimes do fight over something as inconsequential as which television program to watch. In fact, criminologists have long known that when disputes such as this escalate and at times lead to homicide, the reason for one person taking the life of another is often trivial. At the collective level, the issues are generally far from trivial, in particular when the stakes concern access to power and valuable economic resources. Food riots that occur in poor countries when the price of grain forces increases in the price of bread are a case in point.

- Conflicts generally result in the emergence of winners and losers, and the winners are often in a position to control and dominate the losers, thereby perpetuating "patterns of domination and subordination." For example, there is a tendency for competitive markets to move from a number of relatively equal size firms competing on relatively equal terms to a situation of monopoly as some firms are successful in the market while others are not. Success provides financial resources that can be used to drive the competition out of business. The success of Wal-Mart began in rural communities where the big box store competed with locally owned small businesses and in place after place these small operations went out of business. As the dominant retail force in many locales, it was in a position to set the terms of employment—including low wages and aggressive anti-union policies—and could extract from local governments various tax concessions and other benefits.

- The privileged and dominant groups have considerably greater say in deciding how the society should be organized and how resources and power will be distributed. A good example of this is evident in the economic crisis that took hold in the US and UK and spread across the globe. There is considerable consensus that the cause of the crisis was the use of highly complex and risky investment strategies on the part of the largest corporations in the financial sector. They were able to engage in such inherently risky practices because they had used their considerable political influence to implement laws and policies aimed at removing many of the regulatory mechanisms that had been in place, some since the Depression, in order to avert crises from occurring. Despite widespread criticism in the wake of the deep recession that took hold in 2008, key figures in the financial industry continue to shape policy, nobody of consequence has gone to prison, and the very wealthy are again making vast sums of money while middle class citizens continue to struggle with high rates of unemployment and a lack of available credit.

TYPES OF ETHNIC CONFLICT

Sanderson offered a perspective on conflict in general terms. In this chapter, we focus on one specific type of conflict, namely that predicated on race and ethnicity. As the preceding chapter indicated, being defined as a member of a particular group can have very tangible material and nonmaterial consequences for individuals, with the ordinary or average members of advantaged groups possessing distinct benefits compared to ordinary or average members of disadvantaged groups. While our empirical focus in the preceding chapter was on the US, group interrelations predicated on structured patterns of inequality characterize other societies, as well. Advantaged groups have an incentive to ensure that other groups remain subordinate—and are often quite willing to engage in actions intended to ensure their subordinate position. This is what Tilly had in mind in describing exploitation and opportunity hoarding as contributing factors to durable inequality.

When such a social arrangement takes hold, it is not surprisingly a cause of resentment that can give rise to actions on the part of the oppressed and marginalized that are designed to challenge the status quo by either turning the tables on those currently in control or by attempting to promote a society that they consider to be just and equitable.

Across the globe, there has been a dramatic increase in ethnic conflicts within and across nation states in the decades following the major world wars of the twentieth century. As we move further into the twenty-first century, it is clear that race and ethnicity do not only categorize, they also place people in hierarchies that define groups in terms of whether they are to be favored or not, privileged or not, empowered or not, economically advantaged or not, and so forth. This process of dividing people along racial and ethnic lines has frequently resulted in various forms of intra-group conflict, coercion, and violence, including in the most extreme forms of conflict attempts to exterminate an entire group. This chapter will examine several varieties of ethnic conflict, including the following:

- genocide
- ethnic riots
- secession
- **irredentism**
- exclusion

THE ROOTS OF ETHNIC CONFLICT

Milton Esman (2004) makes the obvious point that ethnic conflict can only occur in ethnically plural societies. If a society is ethnically homogeneous (e.g., Iceland until recently), ethnic conflict cannot occur. However, pluralism per se does not lead to conflict. There are many ethnically diverse societies in which groups live in relative harmony.

ETHNIC PLURALISM

Precisely how pluralism was established can, however, speak to the potential for particular types of conflict to emerge. Esman (2004: 51–57) identified five ways in which ethnic pluralism arises:

- Conquest describes a situation in which one ethnic group invades the territory of another, defeats the inhabitants of the territory and takes control of it. The era of colonialism witnessed this phenomenon on a vast scale. Thus, the largest empire to emerge, the British, began by taking control of Ireland and then the areas in North America that would eventually become the United States and Canada, in the first case by defeating the Irish and in the second by defeating the continent's indigenous peoples. In the end, the British Empire encompassed about a fifth of the world's land mass when it could accurately be said that "the sun never set on the British Empire."

- **Annexation** refers to the incorporation of some territorial entity—which can be a nation or a portion of a nation—into another, generally larger, territory. For example, in 1809 Finland was annexed into the Russian empire according to the terms of a treaty Russia entered into with Sweden, which was forced to cede its previous control of Finland. Two more recent examples are the Indian annexation of the small island of Goa off its coast in the Indian Ocean and Indonesia's annexation of East Timor. Near the end of the past century, Saddam Hussein, then the ruler of Iraq, attempted unsuccessfully to annex Kuwait.

- Settler migrations involve the movements of ethnic groups elsewhere. What makes this type of movement distinctive is, in Esman's (2004: 53) words is that it is done "with the intention of establishing permanent residences and assuming control of the area." The two examples he cites involve the Dutch settlers who moved into what became known as South Africa as early as the seventeenth century and Jewish Zionists who in the twentieth century began to settle in Palestine.

- Voluntary immigration refers to the movement of peoples across international borders, generally with the intention of permanent settlement. What makes this type of movement different from settler migrations is that voluntary immigrants are not intent on assuming control of an area. On the contrary, their goal is to seek to become incorporated into the society. The theories of incorporation that will be discussed in Chapter 5 are very much designed to address this particular type of ethnic group. Several countries in the world are largely the result of widespread immigration, and they have come to be known as settler nations. This includes the United States, with the most diverse population in the world, as well as countries such as Australia and Canada. In what is known as the Great Migration, over 50 million people migrated from Europe to the United States during the nineteenth and early twentieth centuries in what has been described as "the largest ever international free movement of people" (King 2010: 28). The current era is also an age of migration, with current estimates putting the number of people living outside their countries of origin at around 200 million.

- Coerced migration occurs when people are forced to move from one territory to another. The Atlantic slave trade that brought 11 million Africans against their wills to North and South America and the Caribbean between the sixteenth and nineteenth centuries represents the largest coerced migration in world history. Another form of coerced migration common during the colonial era was that of indentured labor. Using the British Empire as an example, it used a system of contract labor to compel Indian workers to migrate to places under British control that were experiencing labor shortages, such as Fiji and Trinidad. Yet another type of coerced migrant is the person forced from a nation due to policies of ethnic cleansing. The expulsion of Jews from the Iberian Peninsula in the fifteenth century is an historical case in point, while the flight of Bosnian Muslims in the late twentieth century is a current example. This last example is linked to Esman's final type of coerced migration, which involves refugees: people who have fled their homeland due to the threat of persecution.

COMPETING INTERESTS

There is no one widely accepted theory of ethnic conflict and, moreover, scholars in the field often point out that such conflict has received less theoretical attention than one might have expected. If there is one thing that most scholars agree on today, it is that they dismiss the idea that ethnic conflict is rooted in long-entrenched primordial ethnic identities and relations. An older school of thought, and a view that one can find widely expressed by the person in the street is that ancient animosities are the result of a natural ethnocentrism characteristic of ethnic groups. This perspective tends to treat cultures as unchanging and as playing a highly deterministic role in influencing people's thoughts and actions. The alternatives characteristic of contemporary currents of thought, in contrast, stress the role that interests—both material and ideational—play in generating conflict, specifically when the interests of one group are perceived to be at odds with the interests of another group. Instead of viewing the reasons for ethnic attachments as rooted in deeply held emotional bonds that are rooted in kinship networks, the alternative stresses the more immediate, social reasons for ethnic solidarity within groups and for ethnic conflict between groups.

Built into these various ways in which the establishment of ethnically pluralist societies occurs are different levels of ethnic inequality, defined in terms of access to power and economic resources. Certainly in the cases of conquest and annexation, those doing the conquering and annexing have more power and control of economic resources than the groups that are being conquered or annexed. Though not quite as clear, settler migrants generally have the advantage over the indigenous people they seek to control. In contrast, coerced migrants are at a disadvantage vis-à-vis the members of the receiving society. Most voluntary immigrants are also at a disadvantage, though in the case of what has become known as "brain drain" immigrants—those possessing professional credentials or business acumen—the disadvantages may be either minimal or in some instances non-existent.

In societies where there are power imbalances between ethnic groups, we often, but not always, see class difference between these ethnic groups as well since those with power are able to translate that power into control over a larger share of economic resources. To the extent that this is true, ethnic differences manifest themselves in part as class differences. To study this relationship, Donald Horowitz (1985: 22) compares ethnic groups in societies that contain "ranked groups" versus those that are composed of "unranked groups." In Horowitz's typology, ranked groups represent a hierarchical ordering of ethnic groups along class lines. In situations characterized by the presence of unranked groups, parallel ethnic groups are located side-by-side in the class order. In societies defined by the prevalence of ranked groups, stratification is synonymous with ethnic membership. Horowitz argues that the relationship between ethnic groups and class is important to consider in understanding if, when, and how ethnic conflict arises, develops, and evolves over time. Ethnic conflict can occur within societies organized on the basis of ranked or unranked groups. However, in societies with ranked ethnic groups, the ethnic conflicts are far more likely to fall along class lines, highlighting the differences in material and cultural advantage between ethnic groups.

TYPES OF INTEREST

What are the interests that become, to use Esman's (2004: 75) language, "bones of contention?" Political interests are one of the major interests contributing to conflict. The tactics employed can range from the peaceful to the violent. As an example of the latter, a recent study of civil wars around the world since 1945, Andreas Wimmer, Lars-Erik Cederman, and Brian Min (2009: 334) sought to explain in what conditions armed struggles occurred. They discovered that violent conflicts are more likely in situations where one ethnic group controls the center of power and substantial portions of the population are "excluded from power because of their ethnic background."

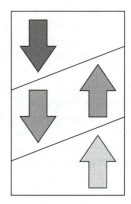 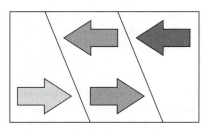

Stratified Society   Ethnically Non-stratified Society

Figure 4.1: Ethnically ranked and unranked societies (drawn by Sabrina Coffey 2011).

A second type of interest revolves around economic interests. An example of competing interests can be seen in the case of the tension between black residents of inner city neighborhoods in several major American cities and Korean immigrant shopkeepers who own businesses in those neighborhoods. In several instances, blacks have organized boycotts and strikes of the businesses, claiming that the merchants charge exorbitant prices and in various ways exploit their customers.

The third type of interest is cultural. The example of black/Korean conflict actually combined both economic and cultural aspects. Part of the tension between the two groups had to do with cultural differences and a lack of intercultural awareness on both sides. From the perspective of many blacks, Korean merchants treated them with disrespect. While political and economic interests revolve chiefly around issues of redistribution, cultural interests are primarily focused on issues of recognition and respect. Put another way, cultural interests are often expressed in terms of identity politics.

Debates over official language policies are a rather widespread instance of culturally based conflict. Demands have been made for elevating the status of minority group languages and for the larger society to assist in protecting the language in many countries. In the developed world, a recent example includes the demands of Québécois nationalists for raising the status of the French language to that of English by defining Canada as officially bilingual. The language question can be found in places in Europe, including in Spain, where both Catalan and Basque ethnonationalists have sought to enhance the place of their respective languages vis-à-vis Spanish.

FIVE TYPES OF CONFLICT

We now turn to the five types of conflict listed at the beginning of the chapter: genocide, ethnic riots, secession, irredentism, and exclusion.

GENOCIDE

Genocide occurs when an attempt is made to exterminate an ethnic group (including groups defined in terms of race, religion, and nationality). The term was coined by legal scholar Raphael Lemkin to account for two mass murders that took place in the first half of the twentieth century, those of Armenians in the Ottoman Empire and the Nazi Holocaust that sought to exterminate European Jewry along and other outsider minority groups such as the Romany. He combined the Greek word *genos*, which can be translated as race or clan, with the Latin suffix *cide*, which means killing.

Some scholars, including Polish-born sociologist Zygmunt Bauman (1992: 156–157), have argued that genocide is a distinctly modern phenomenon in which the target of aggression is a collectivity considered to be degenerate or disease-carrying—in both a biological and a sociocultural sense. This claim is disputed by the fact that mass killings of ethnic groups has occurred throughout recorded history. Esman (2004: 123), for example, cites the case of the Israelite nation that, once it had conquered the Promised Land, set about exterminating the Canaanite tribes. Bauman had in mind the Holocaust, which occurred in a modern industrial nation and was made possible in part by the use of modern technology (e.g., many mass killings took place in gas chambers making use of a manufactured gas called Zyklon B) and modern bureaucratic organizational and managerial practices (e.g., using existing transportation systems to provide a means of getting victims to concentration camps).

Fifty years later, near the end of the past century, another genocide took place, this time in the far poorer and less developed African nation of Rwanda. Although some of the elements of the modern world were employed—particularly the radio, which was a key means for spreading propaganda—many of the features of this mass killing were premodern. The killing mobs generally walked throughout the countryside looking for victims and the operative killing tool was the machete.

Genocides are not the only form of mass murder, and in some instances it is contested whether or not particular acts of violence qualify as genocides. For example, in the 1950s, the Communist Party of China enacted agricultural policies that resulted in mass starvation. It does not appear to have been a deliberate act of killing, but rather one of totally misguided policies combined with an unwillingness to admit error and a cover-up of the most gruesome consequences. Moreover, it does not appear to have been a policy aimed at eliminating a particular ethnic group. In the case of Cambodia under the tyrannical Khmer Rouge regime during the 1970s, the government's "killing fields" were intentional creations, the consequence of a calculated policy designed to return the country to a pristine "original state" in order to create a presumed classless paradise on earth. The horrors perpetuated by the regime were directed at the populace as a whole, with particular vengeance directed at the educated stratum (e.g., people who wore glasses were often singled out as victims). On the other hand, a strong case can be made that acts of genocide occurred in the Balkan conflict in the 1990s and that similar acts are occurring at this writing in the Darfur region of Sudan.

We will describe three genocides spread over the entirety of the twentieth century: the Armenian massacres, particularly those that occurred during World War I; the Nazi regimes campaign of genocide during World War II; and the mass killings in Rwanda near century's end.

THE ARMENIAN MASSACRE

Near the end of the nineteenth century, nearly 2 million Armenians resided in the eastern regions of the Ottoman Empire, in proximity to the Russian Empire. Russia had encouraged Armenians, who were Christian, to press for greater territorial autonomy. Over time, Armenian political parties emerged that were separatist in orientation, leading to growing tension with the Ottoman rulers. Repressive measures were instituted, further fueling the nationalist aspirations of the Armenians that ultimately led to a revolt that was violently repressed. It is estimated that 50,000 Armenians were killed by the Turkish military, with the assistance of Kurdish tribesmen. This was a prelude to what would happen two decades later, in the midst of the chaos of World War I.

Armenians residing in the Russian Empire had taken up arms in support of that regime, volunteering to fight against the Turks. When they began to recruit Armenians living in the Turkey, that government ordered the forced migration of 1,750,000 Armenians under what were seen as extraordinarily extreme conditions intended to ensure the deaths of many deportees. It is unclear how many died in what have been called "death marches," many from starvation and illness. But massacres took place during this period using a variety of means, including mass burnings, drowning, summary executions, and extermination camps.

The Armenian Diaspora has sought for decades to get the nations of the world to concur with its belief that the Ottoman Empire's acts during its final years constitute genocide. At present, over twenty nations—including Canada, France, and Germany, but not the UK or US—have officially concurred that genocide occurred. Scholars have noted its highly organized and systematic character, indicative of considerable planning at the highest echelons of government (Dadrian 1989). There is no agreement about precisely how many Armenians died during 1914 and 1915, with estimates ranging from a low of 600,000 to a high of 1.5 million (this figure includes Armenians from both the Ottoman and Russian sides of the border).

THE HOLOCAUST

The weakness of Germany's political center in the aftermath of the nation's crushing defeat in World War I and the harsh conditions imposed on it by the Treaty of Versailles contributed to a period of political instability, with extremes on the left and right vying for power and battling each other. This is the context in which the National Socialists came to power in 1933, with their leader Adolf Hitler assuming the role of chancellor. A core feature of Nazi ideology was its virulent anti-Semitism, which began to have consequences immediately. Anti-Semitism had a long history in Germany, rooted in both cultural—particularly religious—animosities and economic conflicts. However, anti-Semitism's negative potential did not always manifest itself with the same intensity over history and, during periods of relative tolerance, many Jews had worked hard to assimilate.

Nazi ideology built on this old history of prejudice and added a new twist by making explicit reference to Eugenic thinking and the idea of the racial superiority of true Germans—defined as Aryans—and the degenerate nature of Jews. The latter were defined as enemies of the state, with the distinction being made between these long-term citizens as racial outsiders and what were seen as "pure" or "true" Germans. Jews, quite simply, were treated as having no place in an Aryan nation. They were not alone in being so defined. The Roma, gays and lesbians, and the disabled were also targets of Nazi hostility. But Jews were the largest target. The initial stage did not rely primarily on violence or its threat. Rather, non-Jewish Germans were encouraged to boycott Jewish businesses and legislation was passed that resulted in the firing of all Jewish civil servants and the prohibition of Jews from attending German universities. This stage culminated in the passage of the Nuremberg Laws in 1935 that stripped Jews of their citizenship. In short, they were at that point legally defined as aliens, strangers rather than fellow citizens.

A second, more overtly violent phase began shortly thereafter. Nowhere was this more evident than in the events of November 9, 1938, when 7,500 Jewish businesses, 200 synagogues, and the buildings housing many Jewish organizations were attacked throughout the country, and Jews were attacked (over ninety were killed) and 30,000 were arrested and sent to prison camps. This pogrom, which is a term describing attacks on Jewish communities throughout Europe, became known as Kristallnacht, which is usually translated into English to mean the Night of Broken Glass. Some commentators consider this event to be the official beginning of the genocide that would follow.

When Germany invaded Poland and other nations east of its borders, they killed over a million Jews in those countries. Jews, both in Germany and elsewhere, began to be rounded up and sent to the vast network of concentration camps that the Nazi regime had created. Some of these were slave labor camps; in some facilities brutal medical experiments were conducted on prisoners; and many functioned as death camps in which gas chambers were used to kill on a mass scale. This was the culmination of what the Nazis defined as the "Final Solution." In the end, the most frequently cited estimate of the number of European Jews killed by the Nazi regime from its rise to power in 1933 until its defeat in 1945 is 6 million, a figure representing two-thirds of the Jews in Europe (Hilberg 2003).

It was in the aftermath of this descent into barbarism that the United Nations Convention on the Prevention and Punishment of Genocide came into being, the product of an awareness in many quarters that the international community had done little to stop the mass murder from occurring (its first four key articles are listed in Box 4.1). Moreover, in the postwar years considerable attention was given to the question, How could a civilized nation like Germany have committed such unspeakable acts of savagery? As noted in Chapter 2, the authoritarian personality studies associated with Theodor Adorno and his associates (1950) sought to answer the question in terms of a personality type that would be inclined to scapegoat relatively powerless people, blaming them for the social problems confronting a society, while exhibiting a willingness to obey those in positions of

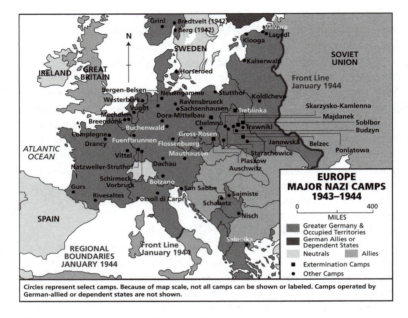

Figure 4.2: Major Nazi camps in Europe, January 1944.

authority. The concern with the personality type inclined to submit blindly to authority was also evident in the famous Milgram "shock experiments" widely familiar to students of introductory psychology classes. Other explanations have focused on such factors as conflict within the society, including more Marxist accounts that defined the conflict in class terms, suggesting, for example, that lower-middle class Germans saw their economic position as increasingly precarious and their status anxiety made them prime candidates for the appeal of Nazi propaganda (Lipset 1960: 145–148).

Without necessarily disputing either the psychological focus of the authoritarian personality argument or the sociological class conflict and status anxiety thesis, other commentators stress that it is important to consider the specificity of the enemies of the Holocaust. In the case of Jews, anti-Semitism was a deeply embedded feature of German culture, a feature that given certain conditions—such as periods of economic and political uncertainty—and the impact of a highly charged and sustained propaganda campaign, could lead to

Box 4.1: United Nations Convention on the Prevention and Punishment of the Crime of Genocide, adopted on December 9, 1948.

Article 1

The Contracting Parties confirm that genocide, whether committed in time of peace or in time of war, is a crime under international law which they undertake to prevent and punish.

Article 2

In the present Convention, genocide means any of the following acts committed with intent to destroy, in whole or in part, a national, ethnic, racial, or religious group, such as:

- Killing members of the group;
- Causing serious bodily or mental harm to members of the group;
- Deliberately inflicting on the group conditions of life calculated to bring about its physical destruction in whole or in part;
- Imposing measures intended to prevent birth within the group;
- Forcibly transferring children of the group to another group.

Article 3

The following acts shall be punishable:

- Genocide;
- Conspiracy to commit genocide;
- Direct and public incitement to commit genocide;
- Attempt to commit genocide;
- Complicity in genocide.

Article 4

Persons committing genocide or any of the other acts enumerated in Article 3 shall be punished, whether they are constitutionally responsible rulers, public officials, or private individuals.

substantial sectors of the population either embracing the idea of the Final Solution or being unwilling to do anything to challenge it. It is in this sense that the historian Daniel Goldhagen (1996) spoke of many ordinary Germans as "Hitler's willing executioners."

The Nazi regime was expert at creating a propaganda apparatus that was intended to shape public opinion in ways that support for Nazi ideology would increase. One aspect of this, in the effort to eliminate the Jewish race from not only Germany, but the rest of Europe as well, was to promote intense anti-Jewish sentiment. Jews were portrayed as conspirators intent on world domination, seen simultaneously as ruthless capitalists and as power-hungry communists. They were depicted as defilers of German women and as destroyers of German culture. They were defined, as Figure 4.3 reveals, as vermin. The purpose of this propaganda industry was to dehumanize Jews, to get ordinary Germans to see them as somehow less than human. This was an essential ingredient in preparing the German population for mass extermination.

Figure 4.3: Nazi anti-Semitic propaganda.

The Nazis were also able to make use of sophisticated bureaucratic structures that were already in place when they took power. Raul Hilberg (2003) contends that the reason that the Nazis succeeded in killing so many people was that they did so with bureaucratic efficiency. Unlike the rage of mob violence that we will turn to below, the Holocaust unfolded with the coolness of bureaucrats following the rules to the letter and obeying the orders of their superiors without question. This was, as Ronald Berger (2002: 13) observes, a case where "[i]instrumental rationality supplanted rage." Instrumental rationality is about action based on objective rules, separated from concerns about morality. Berger offers the following example, "Walter Stier, who booked Jews on the Reichsbahn (German State Railways) so they could be transported to Treblinka, claimed that he did not know that Treblinka was in fact a death camp: 'Good God, no! ... I never went to Treblinka. I stayed in Krakow, in Warsaw, glued to my desk ... I was strictly a bureaucrat!' "

GENOCIDE IN RWANDA

Rwanda is a relatively small nation of 7 million people, located in east Africa. A former Belgian colony, the indigenous population was divided chiefly between two groups, the Hutu and the Tutsi, with a third group, the Twa, constituting about 1 percent of the total population. As in neighboring Burundi, the Hutu constitute a substantial majority of the population—85 percent—while the Tutsi amount to about 14 percent. And as in their neighboring country, despite long periods of relative tranquility between these two groups, both nations have experienced campaigns of genocide. In the case of Burundi, the most violent period erupted in 1972, while in Rwanda genocide occurred in 1994. The events in Rwanda have received considerable media attention, including the film *Hotel Rwanda* (2005), and the focus of scholars. Much attention has been given to the failure of the international community to intervene to stop the violence before it had taken a horrific toll.

The roots of the tension between the Hutus and Tutsis can be traced to the colonial era, when the Belgian rulers placed Tutsis into positions of power, in both the governmental civil service and in the military. The result was that the ethnic divisions in the society were also class divisions. This was, to use Horowitz's categorization, a ranked society. In the post-colonial era, this obdurate fact served as the underlying structural fault line in Rwanda, one that created the basis for future conflict. This is not to say that parties from both ethnic communities did not attempt to find ways of overcoming these divisions by bringing Hutus into government and in other ways elevating their place in the social order. There were leaders from both communities that had sought to mediate and mitigate the tensions between the two ethnic communities In fact, President Juvénal Habyarimana, whose assassination was the key precipitating event in sparking the genocide, was a Hutu, which suggests that this group had access to the centers of political power.

At the same time, there were militant ethnic groups in both communities that sought to exploit the accumulated historical animosities that characterized Hutu/Tutsi relations. The early 1990s saw Rwanda experience economic difficulties as it increasingly confronted a global economy. It was also a period of growing political uncertainty as extremists within the Hutu community began to plan for a takeover of the nation and a campaign to rid the country of its entire Tutsi population. When President Habyarimana's plane was shot down on April 6, 1994, militants had the pretext for unleashing their campaign of terror. Within 100 days, 800,000 Tutsis—men, women, and children—were killed. Lacking the bureaucratic and technological tools that the Nazis had available, the leaders of the genocide made use of propaganda to instill fear in the population, both Tutsi and Hutu alike. The goal was to divide the two communities and to prevent moderate Hutus from dampening the flames of violence. Philip Gourevitch (1998: 96) described what happened in the following passage:

> Yet it was the Germans, not the machinery, that did the killing. Rwanda's Hutu Power [the extremist movement] leaders understood this perfectly. If you could swing the people who would swing the machetes, technological underdevelopment was no obstacle to genocide. The people were the weapon and this means everybody: the entire Hutu population had to kill the entire Tutsi population.

Not only were Tutsis targeted for attack, but Hutus sympathizing with the Tutsis were also killed. Moreover, anyone who sought to avoid participating in attacks on Tutsis was viewed with suspicion. As one of the respondents in Scott Straus' book, *The Order of Genocide*

2006: 136) put it, "Anyone who did not go on a patrol [to seek out and kill Tutsis] paid a penalty. That is where people were killed. The people who killed first, afterward they obliged others to kill."

Although the international community was aware of the genocide from its planning stages through to its bloody conclusion, it did little. Ultimately, the violence ended when a rebel group composed largely of Tutsis defeated the Hutu Power movement and seized control of the country. But by that time, about three-quarters of the Tutsi population had been killed.

ETHNIC RIOTS

Ethnic riots are similar to genocides insofar as the conflict takes violent, indeed often deadly, form. Riots differ from genocide insofar as they typically involve less planning and often have the appearance of a spontaneous event. What is often most evident to the third party observer is the highly charged emotional nature of a riot. Donald Horowitz's (2001: 1) definition nicely summarizes such riots in the following way, "A deadly ethnic riot is an intense, sudden, though not necessarily wholly unplanned lethal attack by civilian members of one ethnic group on civilians of another ethnic group, the victims chosen because of their group membership." We would modify that definition slightly by pointing out that in some ethnic riots the rioters primarily target the property of the other ethnic group rather than persons. Horowitz goes on to note that depending on the context, these are sometimes referred to as "'communal,' 'racial,' 'religious,' 'linguistic,' or 'tribal' disturbances."

The underlying reasons precipitating riots are varied, but share in common a sense of collective grievance. The grievances can be due to a sense that the group has been squeezed out of or placed in a disadvantageous position in the economy—in the labor market, as consumers, and so forth. Or it can be a parallel feeling of disenfranchisement from the centers of political power. It can result from ill-feelings about authority, such as a belief that the police or the courts have been unfair to members of the ethnic group. In the case of immigrants, members of the dominant ethnic group in the receiving society may view the newcomers as a competitive threat or as a challenge to social order, while immigrants may view themselves as the victims of discriminatory practices that put them at a distinct disadvantage as they attempt to gain a foothold in their new homeland.

While the underlying causes of ethnic riots vary, they share in common a certain patterned character to the riot itself. There is a precipitating event, the event that sparks the violence. The mobilization of people relies to a considerable degree on rumors which serve to heighten the sense of collective anger at perceived injustices. Horowitz (2001: 71–102) observes that there is often a lull preceding the riot, a period in which people acquire the emotional state of mind that propels them to violent acts—which includes an intensification of anger and with it a reduction in the fear about the potential consequences of taking part in the violent acts of a riot. Ethnic riots take place in both the developed and underdeveloped nations of the world, though Horowitz thinks that the number of such events taking place in the former is declining. Evidence of the locations of ethnic riots that took place during the first decade of the present century lend credence to Horowitz's assessment. That being said, ethnic riots have not disappeared from developed nations. As illustrations of the rhythm of an ethnic riot, we will briefly examine two riots that occurred in the US, one early in the past century and one during its last decade: the 1919 Chicago Riot and the 1992 Los Angeles Riot.

THE CHICAGO RIOT OF 1919

Northern cities such as Chicago had not implemented the Jim Crow legislation found in southern states that legalized segregation. However, de facto segregation was a reality of everyday life. Chicago was a city built by immigrants in the nineteenth century, but by the early part of the twentieth, blacks from the Mississippi Delta began to migrate to the booming industrial cities of the North, including Chicago. The result was competition between white ethnics— especially the Irish—and blacks in both the labor and housing markets. In a report produced by the Chicago Commission on Race Relations (1922) in the aftermath of the riot, it was noted that a compounding factor was an intensification of violent attacks by white gangs on blacks, including the murder of two blacks several weeks before the riot. It was a widely held belief by many blacks that the police did not adequately protect them from such violence.

The riot broke out on July 27, 1919. The precipitating event took place on a beach on Lake Michigan. This particular beach was not part of the city's parks, but was used by both blacks and whites, though the practice was for one section to be used by whites and another by blacks. When a seventeen-year-old black swimmer drifted into water whites deemed to be their part of the shore line, they began to hurl rocks at the swimmer. Blacks entered the white beach to investigate and assist the youth and fights began. The swimmer drowned, and word spread within the black community that he had been stoned to death. Whether the rumor was accurate or not, it was the event that triggered the riot, which saw whites attacking blacks and blacks attacking whites. Over the course of a five day period, thirty-eight persons were killed (fifteen were white and twenty-three were black) and 537 were injured. In addition to assaults and killings, rioters engaged in acts of arson, with nearly 1,000 people—primarily blacks—made homeless. The police appeared unable or unwilling to bring the violence to an end, something that only happened once the governor sent in the state militia to restore order.

THE LOS ANGELES RIOT OF 1992

South Central Los Angeles is an inner-city black neighborhood with high rates of poverty and an array of attendant problems such as high rates of unemployment, failing schools, a lack of decent and affordable housing, gangs, drugs, and high crime rates. At the same time, in the city as a whole it appeared that strides had been made in race relations as a growing black middle class was evident and the Mayor of the city at the time was its first African American, Tom Bradley (see Chapter 2). Racial isolation among the city's black poor and economic decline in their neighborhoods contributed to the persistence of deeply entrenched inequality, which, in turn, contributed to the disaffection felt by many of the area's residents. Given the problems with crime in South Central, the police were a visible presence and many residents had a tense relationship with them.

This was the structural context in which the 1992 riot broke out. The precipitating event was the verdict in the trial of Los Angeles police officers who had been arrested in the brutal beating of black motorist Rodney King after a high-speed chase. Captured on video by a nearby resident, the beating of King while he was showing no resistance to his arrest was quickly broadcast on national television. Four officers were arrested and tried outside of Los Angeles. When the jury of ten whites, one Latino, and one Asian (but no blacks) returned innocent verdicts for three officers and failed to produce a verdict for the fourth, black rage was vented on the streets of South Central. The riot lasted for six days. Many whites driving through the area were attacked by groups of black residents, with the horrific beating of truck driver Reginald Denny being the most well-known because it was filmed by local television crews.

Before it was finally suppressed by state and federal troops, the riot resulted in 53 deaths, 2,383 injuries, over 3,000 businesses attacked, and $1 billion dollars in property damage. What made this particular riot unique was the fact that many Latinos—poor, inner-city residents like their black counterparts—participated in the rioting. In addition, Korean businesses were particularly targeted for attack, reflecting a long-standing animosity between black residents and Korean store owners. Given this racial dynamic, the riot has been dubbed the nation's first multiethnic riot (Baldassare 1994).

SECESSION

A third type of conflict occurs when an ethnic group with territorial claims attempts to leave an existing nation-state in order to establish a new one. Whereas the two preceding types of conflict are by their nature violent, secessionist movements can be violent or nonviolent. Secessionist ethnic groups are ethnonational, which is to say that they are based on nationalist ideology and a conviction that although they are a nation, they lack statehood, or as Montserrat Guibernau (1999) puts it, they are "nations without states" (see also Connor 1994). The goal of secessionist movements is to create an independent state, with the acquisition of regional autonomy while remaining in the existing nation serving in many instances as a fallback position.

A partial list of recent or current examples of secessionist struggles that have resulted in civil war, armed conflict, and/or terrorism include the following:

- the Nagorno-Karabakh region of Azerbaijan,
- East Timor's successful effort to become independent from Indonesia,
- Eritrea's successful struggle to separate from Ethiopia,
- the conflict in the Georgian region of South Ossetia,

- the guerilla movement of secessionists in the Philippine region of Mindanao,
- Kosovo's partially successful effort to get the world community to view it as an independent country rather than a region of Serbia,
- the protracted terrorist violence of the militant organization ETA in Spain's Basque region,
- Tamil secessionists in Sri Lanka,
- and the ongoing independence movement in Sudan's Darfur region.

In contrast, nonviolent ethnonationalist movements, those that rely on ballots rather than bullets, can be found in the Canadian province of Quebec, the Catalan region of Spain, and in Scotland in the UK. We will look a bit more closely at an example from each type: the Tamil secessionist struggle in Sri Lanka and Québécois separatism in Canada.

SRI LANKA

Formerly the British colony of Ceylon, Sri Lanka is an island off the coast of India composed of four primary ethnic groups: Sinhalese Buddhists, which comprise 74 percent of the total population; Hindu Tamils, the largest minority group at 18 percent; Muslims, which represent 7 percent of the population; and Burghers, a term for European-origin citizens, a very small group comprising less than 1 percent of the population.

In the nineteenth century, during the colonial era, both the Sinhalese and Tamil communities developed nationalist identities, in no small part as a result of resistance to the efforts of Protestant missionaries from Europe to convert the population to Christianity. When independence was achieved in 1948, in the era of decolonization that followed World War II, tensions arose between the Sinhalese majority and minority groups, particularly the Tamils. The Tamil community was concentrated in the north of the island, close to the Indian coast, where a Tamil community also resided, one with which they shared a language with Dravidian roots. Tensions grew over time between the Sinhalese and Tamils over issues of the sort of political representation that the minority would be accorded and over matters of economic development in the Tamil region.

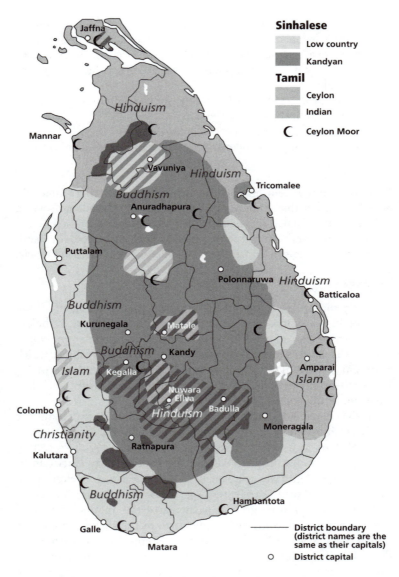

Figure 4.4: Ethnic communities and religions in Sri Lanka.

Both communities had political leaders intent on finding mutually agreeable—win-win—resolutions to the tensions, but within each community more militant organizations also emerged. In the case of Sinhalese extremists, militants were highly critical of what they saw as efforts to pamper the Tamil community, and they sought to define Sri Lankan national identity as an identity that was solely derived from Sinhalese Buddhist culture. Tamil militants argued that the intransience of the Sinhalese majority had effectively disenfranchised the Tamil community, making a case for a secessionist struggle.

Weakness in the society's political center provided the opportunity for extremists on both sides to gain the upper hand over time. In the case of Tamil militancy, it took a violent turn with the creation of the Liberation Tigers of Tamil Eelam (LTTE) in 1972. The armed struggle began with acts of guerrilla terrorism, including extensive use of suicide bombers. By the middle of the 1980s, the LTTE controlled most of the Jaffna Peninsula—the stronghold of the Tamil community—and engaged in acts of aggression in Sinhalese regions of the country, including the nation's capital, Colombo. Their activities only served to further polarize the nation as Sinhalese extremists, with the encouragement of Buddhist monks, pressed for all-out war against the separatists (Bastin 2009).

By the beginning of the current century, the conflict reached an impasse. On the one hand, the Tamil Tigers maintained de facto control of much of the north of the nation. On the other hand, they had not succeeded in becoming a recognized independent state. As the struggle dragged on, they increasingly lost any support they once may have had in international public opinion. In fact, the organization was increasingly characterized as a terrorist organization, which in the "Age of Terror," meant that they found themselves in an increasingly isolated position. For this reason, at one point they proposed a unilateral cease fire, but it did not hold. In the end, the Sri Lankan military undertook a major mobilization in 2008, invading the Jaffna Peninsula, seeking to put down for once and for all the armed insurrection. They succeeded, killing many of the main leadership figures as well as thousands of fighters and innocent civilians. The brutality of the assault has raised questions about war crimes and crimes against humanity.

Over a quarter of a century of warfare did come to an end, a period during which somewhere between 70,000 and 80,000 people lost their lives and countless more were injured. The region, after decades of economic neglect, is impoverished and its infrastructure in a state of disrepair. And a federalist solution that grants considerable regional autonomy to the Tamil community, while the central state invested considerable resources in economic development, has not begun. Nor have substantive attempts to begin the process of reconciliation. Thus, while the violence has at the moment ceased, the conditions that contributed to the conflict persist.

CANADA

Canada, still part of the British Commonwealth, was settled by two competing European peoples, the British and the French. Both are described as "charter" groups involved in the formative period of nation building. However, the British clearly had the upper hand throughout most of Canada, with the Francophone community being heavily concentrated in the province of Quebec. Until the 1960s, most French Canadians lived in a social world isolated from the Anglophone community and lagged behind in terms of such measures as educational attainment, socioeconomic status, political leadership at the national level, and so forth. It is in this context that a separatist movement emerged. The gestation period was known as the "Quiet Revolution." It was characterized by demands to end economic and social discrimination and to increase the political power of the provincial government vis-à-vis the federal state. As such, the Quiet Revolution was more about advancing the civil rights and economic conditions of the Francophone community than in promoting a separatist agenda. However, a key element in the list of demands focused on preserving French culture.

The Canadian government responded by addressing a key aspect of that heritage, the French language. Up to 1970, English was the official language of government and business. Prime Minister Pierre Trudeau pushed through legislation that made Canada an officially bilingual nation. Around the same time the federal government sought in symbolic terms to recast the stature of the two charter groups. For example, it replaced the existing national flag, which was a modified Union Jack that reflected ties to Britain with a neutral flag featuring a red maple leaf. In short, attempts were made to find new common ground between the two charter groups (Evans 1996).

Figure 4.5: Map of Canada.

However, these efforts did not placate many in the Francophone ethnonationalist movement, who over the next three decades attempted to up the ante. Militant separatists described Quebec as an internal colony, and a small minority called for an armed struggle. The embrace of violence proved to be short-lived. Instead, the Parti Québécois sought to raise the independence issue through legitimate political means, seeking to press the federal government for further concessions that would grant greater provincial autonomy, while also preparing the electorate in the province for a referendum on whether to remain a part of Canada. The first vote took place in 1980, at which time it lost by a substantial 60:40 margin. In the aftermath of this defeat, the federal government once again attempted to diffuse separatist sentiment, pressing for what was known as the Meech Lake Accord, which would have kept Quebec in the confederation while according it a status of a "distinct society." A backlash in the other provinces led to a defeat of the Accord. Subsequent efforts were no more successful. Another referendum was held in Quebec in 1995, this time asking voters if they wanted to create a new sovereignty within the context of a partnership with Canada. In an extremely close vote, 50.6 percent of the voters rejected the idea—including an overwhelming majority of both the English-speaking community and new immigrants.

More than a decade into the twenty-first century, the separatist movement has lost ground. This is not to say that separatist sentiment has subsided or will not be a factor to reckon with in the future. What is clear is that some of the factors that underpinned the initial movement in the 1960s no longer hold sway. In particular, the socioeconomic status of French Canadians has improved dramatically during that time and they have found their ways into the corridors of power in Ottawa and in corporate boardrooms. On the other hand, concerns about the future of French culture and language remain a concern.

In short, conflict has not ceased, but it has been institutionalized in ways that maximize respect for the law and for civility in public affairs. This has occurred in a country that is not only prosperous, but works to ensure that inequality—including inequalities at the regional level—are not permitted to get out of hand. Moreover, it works because in Canada, as Jason Kaufman (2007: 587) has observed, "group rights have a strong legal basis and are part of state policy."

IRREDENTISM

Irredentism is a phenomenon that bears a family resemblance to secessionism. It occurs when ethnic groups span national borders and an effort is made to unite them. There are far fewer irredentist movements than secessionist ones (Horowitz 1985: 229). The conditions for irredentism, where they exist in the developing world, have often been due to the map-drawing activities of colonial powers or the international community, particularly when those activities have ignored traditional tribal boundaries. However, one can also find examples in Europe, including Albanian ethnics who live in Serbia and Albania, Hungarians who reside in Hungary and Romania,

Tyroleans in both Austria and Italy, Macedonians in Macedonia and Greece, and the example we turn to: the Irish in Ireland and in Northern Ireland.

NORTHERN IRELAND

Ireland has often been described as Britain's first colony. Indeed, it was controlled by the British until the twentieth century, when Irish nationalism, which began as a cultural movement in the nineteenth century but over time acquired political nationalist ambitions, spawned an independence movement. In a violent struggle that met intense British repression, the Irish achieved gradual and partial independence from Britain. The Anglo-Irish Treaty of 1921 laid the basis for the creation of the Irish Free State, which was largely autonomous, but not fully independent of British rule until the establishment of the Republic of Ireland in 1949. However, less than the entire island was part of this arrangement. The six counties that constituted Northern Ireland remained part of the UK. Whereas Ireland was overwhelmingly Roman Catholic, the six counties differed insofar as the majority of the population was Protestant, the product of past migrations of Presbyterians from Scotland. The sectarian divisions in Northern Ireland revolved around this religious divide, which was further compounded by the fact that Catholics suffered from discrimination in job markets and housing and the "republican" Catholics and "unionist" Protestants lived in separate social worlds. That being said, the class differences between the two communities were not as pronounced as was true in many other settings.

However, by 1970 the conflict had taken on an increasingly zero-sum character. The nonviolent route promoted by the political party Sinn Féin was increasingly criticized and the Provisional Irish Republican Army was born. It became the main Catholic paramilitary organization committed to advancing a violent campaign against continued British rule. The organization's goal was the end of British rule and the reunification with Ireland. The Protestant community responded in kind with the creation of its own paramilitary forces, including the most powerful, the Ulster Defence League (UDL). Thus, the stage was set for a three decade period of interethnic violence known as "the Troubles" in a society that became increasingly polarized over time. The presence of British troops was deemed essential by some (particularly Protestants), while this was seen as an added provocation by the IRA and its sympathizers. During a period of time that largely coincided with the civil war in Sri Lanka, there were about 2,000 deaths in Northern Ireland and elsewhere in the UK.

Neither side had the capacity to achieve their respective goals through violent means. Moreover, the IRA had to contend with the reality that the government of the Republic of Ireland was increasingly indifferent to their desire to end partition. After long and difficult negotiations, mediated in part by former US Senator George Mitchell, a peace accord was signed on April 10, 1998: the "Good Friday Agreement." While small fringe terrorist groups continue to be a problem, since the accord, a slow move toward creating a peaceful resolution to the Troubles has been underway. If this continues, irredentists in Northern Ireland will increasingly resemble their "ballots, not bullets" counterparts in Quebec, Scotland, and Catalonia.

EXCLUSION

Exclusion occurs when a more powerful ethnic group in a nation prevents a less powerful group from entering their territory or forcibly expels it if the group is already there. But it can also occur when the more powerful group renders the less powerful group relatively powerless and marginalized—as either permanent aliens or second class citizens who are prevented from entering the societal mainstream. Exclusion is the most common form of ethnic conflict, one that can occur with or without violence—though if it does so without violence, the powerful groups have the potential for relying on force if they meet resistance from excluded groups. Exclusion is a boundary-defining process, one that determines who is to be seen and treated as an appropriate insider and who is to be seen and treated as being located outside of the societal community's boundaries. Three examples will illustrate each of these types of exclusion.

IMMIGRATION CONTROL

One way to insure that unwanted ethnic groups do not gain entry to a nation is to create laws governing immigration that bar some groups from entry. Due to the hostility of the organized labor movement that viewed them as competitive threats combined with deep-rooted racism that was widespread in the public at large, in the nineteenth century the Chinese constituted the first ethnic group to be so targeted for exclusion. The passage of the Chinese Exclusion Act of 1882 by the US Congress prevented the further entry of Chinese to the nation, and set the stage for further restrictive legislation directed at particular groups. The Gentleman's Agreement of 1907 between President Theodore Roosevelt and the Emperor of Japan, for example, placed severe limits on the number of Japanese that could enter the country. But the native-born opponents of liberal immigration laws did not simply target Asian groups. The much larger numbers of immigrants arriving from eastern and southern Europe during the Great Migration also confronted nativist hostility that took powerful organizational form and ultimately resulted in the passage of the National Origins Act of 1924, which effectively put an end to mass migration for the next four decades.

A parallel development can be found in most of the advanced industrial nations, where public opinion against new immigrants has hardened in recent years—a phenomenon evident in the countries of Western Europe, in the US, in Australia, but not Canada. It can be seen in nations opting to be increasingly opposed to granting entry to new refugees and asylum seekers. None of this has actually succeeded in stopping movement across borders, which raises questions about the extent to which nations are in a position to control their borders. It is in this context that this form of exclusion will likely shape various forms of ethnic conflict for the foreseeable future (Kivisto and Faist 2010: 195–223).

EXPULSION

Forcing ethnic groups to leave a territory where they have settled constitutes another form of exclusionary conflict. The history of the US included the forced movement of American Indians from their traditional tribal lands to places on the western frontier. While not precisely being forced to leave the nation, they were forced out of established states or regions where European-origin ethnics were intent on settling. The result of governmental policies of relocation, which included the creation of the reservation system (a "total institution" in Erving Goffman's (1961) terminology), produced a demographic tragedy as the Indian population was reduced from several million at the beginning of European settlement to a mere 250,000 by 1870.

When the state of Israel was created in 1948 and Jews from Europe and elsewhere in the world chose to settle in the new nation, perhaps as many as a million Palestinians—whose ancestors had long lived in the region—fled or were forced into exile. The largest number of these refugees ended up in Jordan, where refugee camps were created shortly thereafter. Given the fact that the conflict between Israelis and Palestinians remains unresolved after more than a half century, up to this writing the refugees continue to live in these camps under the auspices of the United Nations Relief and Works Agency— amounting to almost a third of the total population of Jordan.

SOCIAL EXCLUSION

The Jim Crow era in the United States and the Apartheid system in South Africa are two particularly prominent examples of racial exclusion and subordination. The former took root first, in the aftermath of the legacy of slavery that ended with the Civil War. Emancipation, despite efforts during the period of Reconstruction in the immediate aftermath of the war, did not pave the way for the incorporation of freed blacks into the ranks of citizenship on equal terms with whites. On the contrary, a new system of racial oppression arose that became known as Jim Crow. It involved two interrelated features: segregation and domination. It operated on the cultural, economic, and political levels. A legal system legitimated this system, but it was backed up by the threat of violence at the hands of terrorist groups such as the Ku Klux Klan. Lynching was a pervasive feature of southern life. Jim Crow persisted for a century, until the Civil Rights movement that emerged in the 1950s and gained its major victories in the following decade, brought it to an end.

In contrast to the US, where whites represent a numerical majority, in South Africa they are a numerical minority. In addition to Indians and "coloreds" (people of mixed race), the largest sector of the population was black. In order to ensure control over this population and exploit their labor while concentrating the nation's economic resources in the hands of whites, the policy of Apartheid (which means "apartness") was promulgated in 1948. It codified a long history of racial oppression by whites of the black majority, thereby formally legalizing segregation and providing the legal basis for insuring the continued impoverishment of the black masses while the white minority was able to live in affluence. As with Jim Crow, Apartheid was resisted by blacks, leading to considerable violence. After a long struggle, the main armed resistance movement, the African National Congress (ANC), finally succeeded in bringing down the racist regime and in 1994 the ANC's leader, Nelson Mandela, was elected president of the nation.

CONCLUSION

This chapter points to the darker side of ethnicity, which is its capacity to be a source of conflict in situations where two or more groups interact with each other. While deeply-rooted historical animosities no doubt play a role in many instances of conflict, it is clearly not true in all cases. Moreover, even when a history of tension exists, the primary factors leading to conflict involve competing interests—both material and ideal. We surveyed five types of conflict: genocide, ethnic riots, secession, irredentism, and exclusion. These are ideal types, which means that concrete instances of ethnic conflict are often a mixture of types, and furthermore, more than one type of conflict can be present at the same time. Implicit in the examples presented is a criticism of those who would suggest that ethnic conflicts are inevitable. To make this claim, it is necessary to rely on essentialist notions of ethnic identity and ethnic relations. In contrast, the social constructionist perspective we subscribe to would have one assume that just as conflicts arise out of the specific actions of actors—individual and collective—in interaction with others, so the elimination, de-escalation, and the taming of conflict by offering it legitimate and civil channels of expression are all possible.

5

MODES OF INCORPORATION

How do racial and ethnic minorities become integrated into the mainstream of society? This is the topic we address in the following pages. As should be clear from the discussion in the preceding chapter, there is nothing inevitable about minority incorporation. Exclusion can persist. Moreover, as we shall soon see, incorporation does not necessarily mean that racial and ethnic groups end up on equal terms with members of the dominant society. Nonetheless, when two or more groups interact over time, their social relations tend to have an impact on group members, shaping the way they view the world and act in it. At present, sociologists primarily make use of three concepts in efforts to describe and assess the dynamics of racial and ethnic relations: **assimilation**, multiculturalism, and—specifically for immigrant groups—**transnationalism**. This trio of concepts will be the focus of the current chapter.

ASSIMILATION

Unlike multiculturalism and transnationalism, which have become significant sociological theories only recently, assimilation has been part and parcel of the conceptual arsenal of sociologists from the formative period of the discipline. Indeed, sociologists began to use the term in the late nineteenth century and it received what is generally perceived to be its canonical articulation at the hands of Robert Ezra Park, one of the prime movers of the famous Chicago School of Sociology nearly a century ago. Until recently, the term was widely used by American sociologists, while their European counterparts have preferred to use different terms with a similar meaning such as inclusion, integration, and incorporation. This has begun to change in recent years, as is evident in a recent comparative study of the assimilation of the children of immigrants in eight European nations (Crul and Schneider 2010). Thus, it appears that we may be heading in the future toward the use of a common language.

THE CANONICAL FORMULATION

Dictionary definitions of assimilation distinguish two interrelated meanings: to make like and to incorporate or bring into. Park thought that both meanings were relevant to the assimilation of racial and ethnic minorities, describing aspects of a social process. According to Park, making like refers to the process by which members of different groups "acquire one another's language, characteristic attitudes, and modes of behavior." Incorporation refers to the inclusion of both individuals and groups into "larger groups" (Park 1914: 606).

THE RACE RELATIONS CYCLE

Much has been made of Park's "**race relations cycle**," which he described on a few occasions as a series of recurring stages of engagement between groups from initial encounter through to the end of the process (Park 1950[1926]). The cycle moved through four distinct stages. The first was *contact*, which takes place on what Park referred to as the "racial frontier," as groups that heretofore had not been in close proximity find themselves in a situation where they need to interact. This stage inevitably gives way to *conflict*, which results because of competition over resources and a desire to control. While overt conflict can persist for a significant period of time, it gives way to *accommodation*, which permits the establishment of a stable social order, but one characterized by power asymmetries characterized by various manifestations of inequality. The stability created during this stage established the conditions for improving intergroup relations over time, leading to the fourth and final stage, *assimilation*, at which point the boundaries that have separated groups break down, not only culturally and socially, but physically as well as widespread intermarriage occurs. The result of the four-stage process is that the original distinct groups disappear as a new, larger homogeneous group takes their place. To call this a cycle may be something of a misnomer, for once the final stage is achieved, the process ends for the two groups in question. It's a cycle only insofar as it presumably repeats itself whenever two groups come into contact with one another.

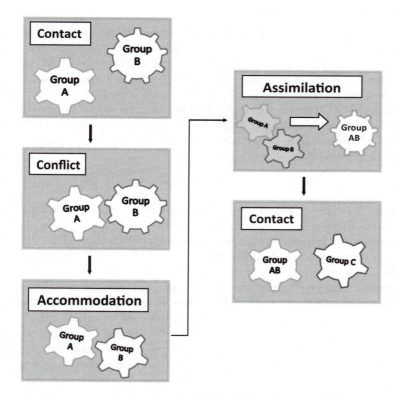

Figure 5.1: Robert Park's race relations cycle (drawn by Sabrina Coffey 2011).

Criticisms of the race relations cycle have come from many quarters, but can be nicely framed by one of the earliest critiques and what is probably the most recent. The former refers to Stanford Lyman's (1972: 27–70) oft-cited essay on the race relations cycle and its implications for an important sociological tradition of race relations research in America. Lyman was critical of what he considers to be its teleological character, or in other words its view of social change as moving toward an inevitable end point. Park, he argued, was part of a larger tendency in American sociology that looked at social life through the lens of evolutionary theory. The net result was that social processes were seen as occurring in a gradual, incremental, directional, and uniform manner. As a consequence, ruled out of consideration *tout court* were the messy contingencies of history and the possibility that different outcomes of intergroup relations were possible.

This criticism dovetails with Stephen Steinberg's recent effort to historicize the very terms Park used to describe the stages of the cycle. Steinberg (2007: 51) describes contact as a "euphemism for colonialism" and competition a "euphemism for conquest and slavery." He goes on to point out that the word "accommodation" conjures up images of compliance and servility in the face of injustice—and, as in the American case of the Uncle Tom (derived from a character in Harriet Beecher Stowe's famous nineteenth century novel, *Uncle Tom's Cabin*, the term coming to be a derogatory characterization of any servile black male), of efforts to curry the favor of the "winners" of the competitive struggle. Assimilation, thus, is a term divorced from the fact that the process of getting there entailed untold suffering and sacrifice, reduced simply to "the price of progress" (Steinberg 2007: 52).

These criticisms of the race relations cycle as a variant of evolutionary thought are on target. And there is certainly a passage in Park's work that provides the critics with a tempting target:

> The race relations cycle which takes the form, to state it abstractly, of contacts, competition, accommodation, and eventual assimilation, is apparently progressive and irreversible. Customs regulations, immigration restrictions, and racial barriers may slacken the tempo of the movement; it may halt it altogether for a time; but cannot change its direction; cannot at any rate, reverse it

> (Park 1950[1926]: 150)

PARK'S VIEW OF RACIAL PROGRESS

Yet a careful reading of Park's work as a whole can lead one to question how significant the race relations cycle actually was to his view of race and ethnic relations in general or assimilation in particular. Indeed, it's worth noting that in the three articles he authored during his lifetime that explicitly addressed what he meant by assimilation he did not make any reference to the cycle (Kivisto 2004). Furthermore, as Lyman (1992: 33) noted two decades after his original commentary on the race relations cycle, by the 1930s Park had begun to have second thoughts about the idea of social change occurring in an evolutionary fashion.

Certainly, he was unconvinced that blacks in America were likely to be assimilated in the foreseeable future, and he was keenly aware that the initial contact between blacks and whites in the US occurred in the seventeenth century—three centuries earlier. Finally, Park was not a rosy-eyed optimist who blithely ignored what Steinberg above called the "price of progress." In "An Autobiographical Note," he wrote that, "I knew enough about civilization even at that time [when he was working as a muckraking journalist for the Congo Reform Association] to know that progress, as philosopher William James once remarked, is a terrible thing. It is so destructive and wasteful" (Park 1950[1926]: vii).

In short, Park thought that assimilation was a powerful, but not an inevitable social process. He was well aware of the many barriers that marginalized and oppressed groups confront in their quest to become equal members of the larger society.

THE RESEARCH LEGACY

Park and the generation of Chicago School sociologists he trained were acutely aware of the fact that the barriers to assimilation were significant and though not necessarily eternal, had real durability. At the same time, they thought that the American society they were studying during the first half of the twentieth century did show signs of change. A major preoccupation in their research agenda concerned explorations of the persistence of social and spatial distance between groups.

RESEARCH TOOLS

Two of the most well-known research tools that came out of the Chicago School were the **social distance scale**, created by former

Park student Emory Bogardus (1933), and the concentric zone model of urban residential patterns. The former allowed generations of sociologists to query people about their willingness to interact at various levels with members of different ethnic groups, with questions ranging from whether members of a particular group should even be permitted to enter the country to at the other end of the spectrum whether a person would be sympathetic to their child marrying a person from the group. Box 5.1 lists the seven questions people were asked regarding their willingness to accept members of various racial and ethnic groups, along with the scores they received for each answer. A score of 1 indicated little or no social distance, while at the opposite end a score of 7 revealed an extreme social distance.

Box 5.1: Bogardus' social distance scale.

Would you accept people from group X:

- As close relatives by marriage (1.00)
- As close personal friends (2.00)
- As neighbors on the same street (3.00)
- As co-workers working alongside you (4.00)
- As citizens of your country (5.00)
- As visitors to your country (6.00)
- Or would you exclude them from your country altogether? (7.00)

The latter, deriving from the social ecology perspective promoted by Park, provided the initial basis for demographic studies that sought to determine levels of residential segregation by race. One such outgrowth is the index of dissimilarity, which despite some built-in shortcomings, continues to be a widely used index for ascertaining levels of segregation (Iceland 2009). Thus, we know by using this index that at this writing, Chicago—the "laboratory" for the Chicago School—continues to be one of the most segregated of the major cities in the US. For information on how the index is calculated, see Box 5.2, which is a concise description that appears on the website of the Racial Residential Segregation Measurement Project at the University of Michigan's Population Studies Center.

Box 5.2: The index of dissimilarity.

The most commonly used measure of neighborhood segregation is the *index of dissimilarity*. This is a measure of the <u>evenness</u> with which two groups are distributed across the component geographic areas that make up a larger area. For purposes of census taking, metropolises are divided into census tracts that contain, on average, about 4,000 residents. We could consider a metropolitan area such as Los Angeles and determine the evenness with which whites and blacks are distributed across census tracts.

One extreme possibility would be an American Apartheid situation in which all blacks lived in exclusively black census tracts while all whites lived in all-white census tracts. Of course this does not occur but this would be the maximum residential segregation of blacks from whites. If there were such an apartheid situation, the *index of dissimilarity* would take on its peak value of 100. Another extreme example would be a situation in which blacks and whites were randomly assigned to their census tracts of residence. This never happens but, if it did, the *index of dissimilarity* would equal 0 meaning that blacks and whites were evenly distributed across census tracts.

In metropolitan Los Angeles in 2000, the *index of dissimilarity* comparing the distribution of blacks and whites across census tracts was 69 indicating a moderately high degree of residential segregation. This value reports that either 69 percent of the white or 69 percent of the black population would have to move from one census tract to another to produce a completely even distribution of the two races across census tract; that is, an *index of dissimilarity* of 0.

Population Studies Center, University of Michigan

RACE AND ETHNICITY IN YANKEE CITY

Perhaps the most important work to emerge from the original Chicago School tradition was W. Lloyd Warner and Leo Srole's *The Social Systems of American Ethnic Groups* (1945), which was part of their Yankee City studies. Both methodologically and theoretically their work was emblematic of a tradition of sociological research that extended into the 1960s. This was a major study of Newburyport, Massachusetts, a medium-sized city in the Boston orbit. Warner and Srole sought to offer a panoramic overview of all of the varied groups in the city, dividing them into three categories: ethnic, racial, and ethno-racial (a rather vaguely defined middle category).

They sought to ascertain which groups were likely to assimilate relatively quickly and which groups would face a much slower process of inclusion—with no guarantees of an outcome similar to those who assimilated quickly. To that end, they developed a "scale of subordination and assimilation." Not surprisingly, they concluded that ethnic groups from Europe who were defined as white were assimilating rather quickly, while racial minorities, especially blacks, confronted a major obstacle to assimilation insofar as they were forced to exist in a static caste social location while others found themselves in a fluid class social structure. In short, assimilation for some groups appeared to be almost a given while for others it appeared to be extremely unlikely well into the future. The interstitial category proved to be more ambiguous or uncertain, though they had some ideas of the direction. Thus, they argued that Asians would likely end up in a "semi-caste situation," while Latinos could conceivably end up in either a class or caste location.

THE THEORY REFINED

Assimilation is clearly a multidimensional phenomenon, a fact that was not always captured by sociologists influenced by the canonical formulation. A half century after Park's initial formulation, Milton Gordon (whose embrace of the ideal of assimilation was personal, having changed his given name from Milton Meyer Goldberg to Milton Myron Gordon in the 1940s) published what proved to be an influential study, *Assimilation in American Life* (1964). The rationale for the book was to provide the reader with an empirical stocktaking of the state of assimilation in a nation built by immigrants, but which had not experienced a major migratory wave since the passage of anti-immigration legislation in 1924. Thus, it was not an effort at theory construction.

GORDON'S TYPOLOGY

However, what was original about the book and what continues to make it a landmark work was the typology of assimilation that it presented. Gordon (1964: 71) identified seven different types of assimilation:

- *Cultural or behavioral assimilation,* which he also described as acculturation, harks back to Park's idea of assimilation as "making like." It refers to a situation in which members of different ethnic or racial groups share a common language, values, folkways and mores, and a general worldview (e.g., one that emphasizes individualism versus collective attachments).
- *Structural assimilation* refers to social integration, which occurs in several areas of social life. This includes residential, educational, and occupational integration. It is also the inclusion of previously excluded groups from membership in such institutions as voluntary associations and fraternal organizations. In addition, it involves the breaking down of barriers to public facilities such as trains, buses, parks, hospitals, and so forth.
- *Marital assimilation* is achieved when the choice of marital partner is not predicated solely on the selection of ingroup options, but rather is equally open to members of other groups. This type of assimilation is often referred to as amalgamation, because it represents the physical breaking down of group boundaries, resulting in multiethnic and multiracial offspring. Like Park, Gordon thought that this was the most difficult type of assimilation to achieve.
- *Identificational assimilation*—a somewhat awkward term —points to the type of assimilation that occurs when members of different groups develop a shared sense of peoplehood at the societal level. This category is obviously related to cultural assimilation, but is nonetheless analytically distinct. It points to an assimilation in which group differences can persist, but don't hinder the prospect of a shared identity despite differences. The powerful feeling of being an American in the immediate aftermath of 9/11, and the parallel sense that many British citizens felt in the wake of the 7/7 bombings illustrate what Gordon meant by this type.
- *Civic assimilation* is similarly connected to both cultural and identificational assimilation. In this form of assimilation, interethnic conflicts over values and power are overcome by a shared identity predicated on citizenship. In other words, in everyday life in modern societies, people assume a variety

of distinct roles, including their ethnic and racial roles, and citizenship is one of those roles. Moreover, it is not simply one among several competing roles, but can become a major source of social harmony and in the process tamping down the potential for ethnic tension and conflict.

- *Attitude receptional assimilation* is a distinctive way of saying that there is a lack of prejudice or at least a very low level of prejudice such that negative attitudes and stereotypes of particular groups no longer constitute an impediment to incorporation.
- *Behavioral receptional assimilation* is the counterpart to the preceding type, in this case involving the absence or low level of discrimination that is sufficient to eliminate this barrier to full inclusion into society.

One of the virtues of this typology is that it allows for an ability to distinguish between different facets of assimilation and to see that it is possible to find evidence of assimilation in some types and little assimilation in other. Thus, blacks are by most measures culturally assimilated (e.g., they speak English and are predominantly Christian), but often live in highly segregated neighborhoods and send their children to equally segregated schools.

"THE KEYSTONE IN THE ARCH"

Although Gordon did not attempt to develop the typology into a coherent theoretical model, he did at least suggest in part how these types were connected. In his view, cultural assimilation was more readily achieved than structural assimilation, with marital assimilation posing an even greater challenge. While he did not propose a uniform process, or contend that assimilation writ large was inevitable, he did see certain tendencies in American society that served to promote assimilation. One thing was clear to him: structural assimilation was the most crucial. As he put it, "Structural assimilation, then, rather than acculturation, is seen to be the keystone in the arch of assimilation." In other words, if structural assimilation was achieved, the rest would follow. As the example of blacks noted above indicates, such is clearly not the case with cultural assimilation.

EVIDENCE OF ASSIMILATION: WHITE ETHNICS

Recall that back in the 1940s, Warner and Srole thought that assimilation was occurring rapidly for white ethnics, immigrants or the descendants of immigrants from Europe, while it was in many regards stymied for blacks and some other racial minorities. Here we examine the first part of this claim and in the following section we turn to the second.

The question can be simply put: have white ethnics assimilated? The answer is "no" if by assimilated we mean that group boundaries have been eradicated as individuals have come out of the melting pot, their previous ethnic identities having disappeared. But it is worth noting that neither Park nor Gordon thought that assimilation necessarily led to this result. Indeed, in Gordon's case, he actually thought that assimilation and what he called "**cultural pluralism**" could coexist.

This was not what some cultural pluralists during the 1960s and 1970s thought. In their view, any evidence of ethnic persistence meant that assimilation had not occurred and was not occurring. These were what became known during the era as the "unmeltable ethnics." There was a good deal of mixing of empirical analysis with social agenda by advocates of what was dubbed an "ethnic revival" among European-origin ethnics. Whether motivated by a desire to preserve the heritages of particular ethnic groups or by a reaction to what were perceived to be gains by blacks at the expense of working class whites in the wake of the civil rights movement, the ethnic revival had its moment in the sun. Its short history need not concern us here. What is of interest is whether there was evidence to support the claim of some cultural pluralists that assimilation was not occurring.

GREELEY ON CULTURAL PLURALISM

In this regard, the key figure associated with this claim is the sociologist (and priest) Andrew Greeley. Making use of data from the National Opinion Research Center, which captured elements of attitudinal and behavioral features of subjects that might reveal the persistent impact of ethnic heritage, he sought to determine the extent to which cultural background had an impact on a variety of personality traits. He hypothesized, for example, that because they were more religious than Italians, the Irish would provide evidence of being more trusting. In this particular example, the evidence did not support the hypothesis. What Greeley found overall was a very mixed bag, leading him to offer the following highly qualified summation, "to some extent some dimensions of the ethnic culture do indeed survive and enable us to predict some aspects of the behavior of the children, grandchildren, and great-grandchildren of immigrants" (Greeley 1974: 319).

Interestingly, Greeley didn't mention the fact that structural assimilation appeared to be occurring as ethnic institutions were disappearing along with the use of the ancestral language and ethnic enclaves were being vacated for multiethnic suburbs. Moreover, marital assimilation had become increasingly commonplace. Granted, his data did not provide evidence of these aspects of assimilation, but it is curious that he doesn't try to connect in some fashion cultural assimilation to Gordon's "keystone." The result is that while Greeley was able to illustrate evidence of some persisting patterns of ethnic culture manifested in personality traits, he fails to offer a framework for understanding what it means and how persistence is connected to counterevidence pointing to assimilation.

SYMBOLIC ETHNICITY

Such an interpretive frame was provided by Columbia University sociologist Herbert Gans (1979), who described the ethnic allegiances of European-origin ethnics as expressions of "**symbolic ethnicity**." What he meant by this term is that many ethnics no longer were prepared to live by all of the normative expectations required by traditional allegiance to their ethnic group's culture, but rather were intent on holding on to their ethnic identities, periodically and selectively, primarily for reasons of nostalgia.

Two complementary studies lent considerable credence to Gans' idea that assimilation was occurring, both appearing in 1990: Richard Alba's *Ethnic Identity* and Mary Waters' *Ethnic Options*. Alba's study was based on interviews of a random sample of 524 residents of the Capital Region of New York state, while Waters' project entailed in-depth interviews of sixty white ethnics of European descent who were also Roman Catholic from a California suburb and Philadelphia, relying on snowball sampling. Both researchers concluded that ethnicity no longer has the same impact on such factors as educational and occupational choice or marital selection as it once did. However, this did not mean that these ethnics found no meaning in their ethnic identities. To the contrary, ethnicity continued to resonate subjectively with their subjects, though as Waters' title indicated, it was embraced in a highly selective manner as people opted to pick and choose from among their ancestral cultural traditions.

WHO CHANGES?

As the descriptions of key assimilation studies from the 1940s to the 1990s reveals, the focus of research is on ethnic minorities, and not on the larger society. The assumption is that in the process of becoming more alike entails the transformation of members of these groups. Unexplored is whether or not the majority or the mainstream changes in the process of interaction over time with ethnic minority groups. Borrowing from a schema proposed by William Newman (1973), we can examine four possible outcomes of intergroup social relations.

ANGLO-CONFORMITY

The first possible outcome can be characterized in the following formula:

$$A + B + C \rightarrow A \text{ (where A is the dominant group)}$$

In such a scenario, A would represent the Anglo-American in the US context, while B and C might represents Italians and Mexicans. Here the change that occurs over time is that Italians and Mexicans take on the attitudinal and behavioral characteristics of the English-origin dominant group. In its most pristine form, as the above suggests, this would result in the total loss of Italian and Mexican identities as they became amalgamated into the large Anglo-American pot. We have indicated that the empirical evidence does not support this picture.

UNCHANGING CULTURAL PLURALISM

However, neither does it support the opposite perspective, which suggests that somehow after a considerable period of intergroup relations, the groups manage to persist unmarked by their encounter with others, as the following would indicate:

$$A + B + C \rightarrow A + B + C$$

As the research from those seeking to explore the extent to which cultural pluralism was a fair description of American society reveals, nothing like this outcome has occurred.

AMERICANIZATION

This leads to the question: if neither dramatic change for minority groups leading to their elimination nor a lack of change for all groups has received empirical confirmation, what does the picture look like? How would we define it? One possibility would be to go further than the first model above and claim that all groups are so radically transformed that the end result is a qualitatively new identity for all concerned, as the following would suggest:

$$A + B + C \rightarrow D$$

Again, there is no evidence that anything so dramatic had occurred. If it had, one might think that Americans would have abandoned English for Esperanto and Christianity for Baha'i or an original New Age religion!

PLURALIST ASSIMILATION

We believe that the evidence on hand, and there is a voluminous body of work that has explored immigration to America from colonial times to the present as well as an equally substantial body of work on the black experience and a smaller though not insubstantial research tradition on Native Americans, calls for a conceptual perspective that appreciates two facts. First, intergroup relations have been characterized by both change and persistence. Second, all groups have to some extent been transformed by their encounters with other groups—the majority group and all minority groups. Precisely how this might be captured schematically is a somewhat open question. One possibility, the one we find most convincing, would be as follows:

$$A + B + C \text{ (the dominant group)} \rightarrow ACD + BCD + CD$$

What this diagram indicates is a society in which discrete ethnic groups do not disappear, but are transformed in the process of intergroup interaction over time. The result of that interaction is that they come to share a common identity that, in the best of situations, exists harmoniously with particularistic ethnic identities. The common identity in question is an overarching national identity. It is not the case that each group in the society has an equal impact on the social construction of that national identity. Rather, groups that are large, have long histories in the society, and have played a dominant role in that society will have a larger impact than groups that are small, have arrived recently, and have entered the society as marginalized and often oppressed members. Nevertheless, the assumption is that the net result is a national identity that does not simply reflect the image of hegemonic groups.

SEGMENTED ASSIMILATION

Until recently, when speaking about assimilation, it was assumed that it involved entry into something called "the mainstream." As it turns out, this is a remarkably undefined concept, as Roger Waldinger (2003) has recently observed. It can be assumed to refer to entry into the middle class, where people share a basic standard of living, life style, and opportunities for advancement. Research clearly reveals that this sort of assimilation does occur in a majority of cases in societies, such as the US and UK, where the middle class constitutes the largest and most diverse class in the society. Nevertheless, there are others who change as a result of their encounter with members of other groups, but the change that occurs does not land them in the mainstream.

THE THEORY OUTLINED

Recently, Alejandro Portes, working with various colleagues, has advanced the idea of **segmented assimilation** to account for this phenomenon (see Portes and Zhou 1993). While this may have been an appropriate concept to use in discussing immigrants from the past, the argument has been specifically developed with contemporary post-industrial economies in mind. In the past, the manufacturing sector, particularly as it unionized, provided a vehicle for new immigrants to improve their economic circumstances and positioned them to pursue the goals and aspirations of the middle class, such as homeownership and university educations for their children. In short, it became a way for newcomers to gain entrée to the middle class.

Since the deindustrialization of the major capitalist economies that took off in the 1970s, the number of unionized manufacturing jobs has decreased dramatically, thus closing off this avenue to upward mobility. Portes argues that the resulting capitalist economies have come to resemble an hour glass, with a lot of low-paying, temporary, non-unionized jobs that do not easily translate into moving up in the organization from the bottom and similarly a lot of white collar professional jobs at the top, jobs that have human capital requirements (e.g., educational credentials) lacking in those located in the economy's bottom tier. As an alternative to involvement in the larger economy, one economic option for some ethnics is to find work among fellow ethnics in the niche or enclave economy. While this is sometimes preferred over working in a lower tier job in the larger economy, such work does not easily or readily translate into enhanced opportunities for advancement.

One of the things that is readily apparent among contemporary immigrants is that there is a considerable division between those with low and those with high levels of human capital. Thus, in the US, one finds large numbers of Mexican immigrants who have not earned high school diplomas working as itinerant laborers in the country's agricultural fields or in sweat shops, while on the other hand many Indians who have arrived during the past two decades come with advanced degrees in medicine or science and technology, and they have found themselves quickly obtaining well-paying, high status jobs.

Segmented assimilation concentrates on examining the ways that the children of newcomers in the bottom tier end up confronting three serious obstacles: racial discrimination, a bifurcated labor market, and inner-city subcultures (Portes and Rumbaut 2001). Their everyday interactions are far more likely to occur with poor inner-city blacks than with affluent suburban whites, and it is the former that comes to play a significant role in shaping the acculturation process. John Ogbu (1978) has argued that many inner-city black youths have embraced an oppositional culture that distains being white. Yale University ethnographer Elijah Anderson (2000) has referred to this adversarial lifestyle as defined in terms of the "code of the street." The segmented assimilation thesis contends that when dissonant acculturation occurs, it can readily lead to downward mobility, which contributes to such counterproductive behaviors as gang involvement, drug activities, unplanned pregnancies, and dropping out of school.

CRITICAL ASSESSMENT

Some critics of segmented assimilation theory argue that it paints too negative and stark a portrait and tends to overemphasize the role that race plays in the process. No serious scholars appear prepared to argue that downward mobility due to dissonant acculturation doesn't occur, but they do question how extensive it is while also pointing to the fact that native-born whites can also embrace an oppositional identity (see, for example, Kasinitz, *et al.* 2008). While the focus of research on segmented assimilation has been the US, some research on other nations has been produced, yielding mixed results (Boyd 2002; Silberman, *et al.* 2007).

Despite some problems with segmented assimilation as it is currently understood, it has the virtue of attempting to connect the acculturation patterns of various ethnic groups to their differing social class locations. While assimilation theory at the hands of Park and his followers paid very little attention to social class, even with Gordon's call for consideration of what he dubbed "ethclass," this is a positive development—one that represents less of a break with the tradition of assimilation theory than a useful corrective to it.

MULTICULTURALISM AS A NEW MODE OF INCORPORATION

It's a truism to say that the world's major advanced industrial nations have in recent decades become increasingly diverse societies. The assertiveness of long-marginalized indigenous peoples (e.g., the Native Americans in the US, First Nations people in Canada, Australia's Aborigines, and the Sami in northern Finland, Norway, and Sweden) has helped to make diversity increasingly visible. The same can be said of the movements of **ethnonationalist minorities** for greater autonomy or even independence (e.g., the Scots and Welsh in Britain, the Basques and Catalan in Spain, and the Québécois in Canada). Finally, the third factor contributing to growing diversity is immigration. Indeed, despite deep ambivalence and often with considerable levels of opposition, these nations have become countries of new immigrants. This includes large numbers of immigrants from Turkey in Germany, Muslims from northern Africa in France, Afro-Caribbeans and Asians from the Indian subcontinent in Britain. It includes large contingents of Chinese and Indians in Canada, and similarly large numbers of Mexicans, Chinese, Koreans, and Indians in the US. It also includes much smaller numbers of a wide array of ethnic groups in all of these nations and in similar ones.

MULTICULTURALISM AND ITS CRITICS

In many instances, when people seek to depict a society as diverse, they use as a synonym the term multiculturalism. Ever since the word entered the vocabularies of ordinary people and multiculturalism became a reality, it has had its vocal critics. In the US, this includes such figures as the late historian Arthur Schlesinger, Jr. (1992) and the sociologist Todd Gitlin (1995). Both feared that multiculturalism, not as a description of diversity, but as what they perceived to be a political agenda, was divisive. The former was concerned about the "disuniting of America," while the latter feared that we might be entering the "twilight of common dreams."

More recently, the late Samuel Huntington, who had been a professor of political science at Harvard and was a key spokesperson for the view that the profound differences between the West and elsewhere, but especially the Muslim world, was leading to a "clash of civilizations." In his last work, *Who Are We?* (2004), he explored what he had concluded was the contemporary threat to American national identity. In his view, the US was historically a nation that assimilated its newcomers through a process known as Americanization. By this, he meant that those who were assimilating were inclined to embrace the fact that the society was defined chiefly by its historic roots, which included the dominance of Protestant Christianity, the English language, and undivided (i.e. not dual) citizenship). What we've just described about critics of multiculturalism has focused on the US. Suffice it to say that similar criticisms have been heard in all of the other countries of North America and Western Europe, as well as in Australia and New Zealand.

PHILOSOPHIES OF MULTICULTURALISM

In the waning years of the past century, Harvard sociologist Nathan Glazer (1997) contended that "we are all multiculturalists now." This is a bold claim given that even two decades earlier there was actually very little use of the term itself. More recently, Yale social theorist Jeffrey Alexander (2006) has presented a sustained case for viewing multiculturalism as a new mode of incorporation, and as such, as a new alternative to assimilation. Is Glazer correct? Is Alexander?

To answer these two questions requires defining multiculturalism, which is a difficult task for two reasons. First, it is used in a rather wide variety of ways, resulting in people frequently talking past each other. Not only are misunderstandings easy, but there are different versions of multiculturalism, with some offering "harder" varieties and others "softer" positions. Second, multiculturalism has proven to be highly controversial, being accused of fomenting societal fragmentation and intensifying ethnic identities at the expense of promoting the common good and shared ideas transcending ethnic boundaries (see, for example, Huntington 2004).

While we disagree with these criticisms, it is not difficult to see where they come from insofar as what makes assimilation and multiculturalism different—both as philosophical positions and political projects—is that the former concentrates on the matter of bringing individuals from heretofore outsider groups into the larger society (call it the mainstream or something else), while the latter is concerned with finding ways to make a virtue of diversity. Indeed, multiculturalism begins with the conviction that people of diverse cultural identities cannot be treated as equals in civil society if that which makes them distinctive is ignored. In other words, multiculturalism is concerned with the prospects of finding common ground while simultaneously valuing rather than ignoring cultural differences.

This needs to be qualified somewhat. Our view of multiculturalism dovetails with a number of key theorists, the most important being the Canadian philosophers Charles Taylor and Will Kymlicka, the British social theorists Bhiku Parekh and Tariq Modood, and the American theorist Jeffrey Alexander. All are intent on finding ways to "achieve diversity." By achieving diversity, all of these theorists, despite their differences, seek to preserve and enhance distinctiveness while at the same time expanding the sphere of solidarity to encompass members of other groups. In so arguing, they represent softer or more moderate versions of multiculturalism, in contrast to, for example, the harder or more radical view of the late University of Chicago philosopher Iris Marion Young.

RADICAL MULTICULTURALISM

Young's (1990) position called for the creation of what she called "differentiated citizenship." This type of citizenship places a premium on group differences, including distinctive group rights. She repudiates the idea of universally shared values and worldviews, contending that all they amount to is a projection of the values and worldview of any society's dominant group. In other words, from her perspective, any effort to arrive at a sense of common purpose and a shared identity is inevitably assimilationist, a form of incorporation resulting from socially excluded groups becoming integrated by embracing the values of the dominant group.

Her position has been subject to widespread criticism on the part of soft multiculturalists. Some have pointed out that her understanding of who in the US qualifies for differentiated rights is so broad that something like 75 percent of the population would qualify, including but not simply limited to the main racial minorities in the society, women, gays and lesbians, and members of the working class. What she does in making this case is to treat the idea of culture so loosely that where she sees distinct cultures others would perceive variations within a culture. Beyond this, what serves to distinguish Young's version of multiculturalism from more moderate positions is that it promotes group insularity and social fragmentation. It does so because it fails to reckon with the fact that most people are capable of seeing both the distinctive perspective of their own group and at the same time understand the limits of that perspective and the virtues of also seeing things from the vantage of the larger society. Alexander (2006: 398) has criticized Young for promoting a philosophic position that calls for "recognition without solidarity," by which he means that in claiming to be respected and accorded distinctive rights, members of the groups in question do not in the end establish bonds of attachment and allegiance to members of other groups.

MODERATE MULTICULTURALISTS

While the moderate multiculturalists cited above have all developed original theoretical statements, for our purposes the similarities among these thinkers are far more important than the differences. To begin with, in contrast to Young, they see multiculturalism as a mechanism for including the members of groups that have heretofore been socially excluded. Alexander (2006: 450–457) depicts multiculturalism as a new mode of incorporation, and insofar as this is the case, it represents an alternative to assimilation. Likewise, Modood (2007: 14) describes multiculturalism as "a form of integration."

Multiculturalism does not refer to a social process of group interaction, but rather to a moral choice, one predicated on the idea of recognition. Taylor (1992) is perhaps the most important of the multiculturalists to advance the claim that multiculturalism ought to be construed as a preferred mode of incorporation because unlike assimilation it takes seriously the idea that people's cultural backgrounds constitute an integral element of their sense of self. Because of this it is reasonable to conclude that creating an opportunity to have one's cultural identity recognized in public by others represents a just and equitable way to approach difference. As such, it constitutes a politics of identity, one committed to the promotion of cultures of authenticity.

MULTICULTURAL POLICIES

Posed at the level of philosophy, it is difficult to get a sense of what multiculturalism "on the ground" would look like. At a less abstract level, such as the level of public policy, how should we define multiculturalism? Summarizing the position of Will Kymlicka (1995), Duncan Ivison (2010: 2) contends that it refers to "policies designed to provide some level of public recognition, support, or accommodation to non-dominant ethnocultural groups" (which includes immigrants, refugees, ethnonational minorities, and indigenous peoples). From Kymlicka's perspective, multiculturalism goes beyond the protection of the basic civil and political rights guaranteed to all individuals in a liberal-democratic state, to also extend some level of public recognition and support for ethnocultural minorities to maintain and express their distinct identities and practices.

To speak about public policy means that the nation-state undertakes concrete initiatives to insure that such recognition and support are promoted. This being the case, it is quite obvious that governments would not be interested in advancing the sort of multiculturalism advocated by Young since public officials would be, understandably, concerned that they would lead to fragmentation. In other words, governments have an interest—a self-interest—in facilitating integration and in avoiding fragmentation. Thus, to the extent that any particular government actually promotes multi-culturalism, it will be a version that resembles the perspective of the soft multiculturalists.

Nowhere is this more evident than in Canada, which is the first of the advanced industrial nations to pass legislation that established the nation as officially multicultural (Australia, modeling itself after Canada, was the only country to follow this lead). Some other countries can reasonably be seen as supportive of multiculturalism, including the US and UK, despite the fact that they have not passed an official multicultural act. Rather, these nations exhibit a multicultural sensibility. At the same time, other countries have proven to be quite resistant to multiculturalism, including France among Western European nations and Japan.

CANADA'S OFFICIAL MULTICULTURAL POLICY

Given Canada's status as the nation with the most explicit and robust version of multiculturalism, it is worth highlighting how this came to be and what it means in practice. As is the case with settler nations, Canada's population has been diverse throughout its history and with recent waves of immigration it has become even more diverse. Of significance here is that the nation has been controlled for much of its history by settlers from Britain, and as a consequence has been forced to address the concerns and claims of the indigenous peoples— the First Nations peoples—as well as those of French-speakers concentrated in the province of Quebec. Add to this the so-called Third Force—immigrants from countries other than Britain and France—and the full complexity and diversity of the Canadian mosaic is evident.

Canada's history of multiculturalism involves two stages of development once the country abandoned "assimilation" for "integration." It was triggered by two interrelated events that emerged during the 1960s. The first, the rise of a separatist movement within Quebec's Francophone community, was the most threatening to Canadian society insofar as if successful, it would have resulted in the splitting of Canada into two geographic regions divided by an independent Quebec. This movement was motivated by two major concerns, the economic and political marginalization of the French by the English and the future of the French language and culture brought about by the hegemony of the nation's British heritage. Compounding the challenge confronting the Canadian government was the fact that other immigrants, be they older immigrant stock who arrived in the country during the late nineteenth and early twentieth centuries or were among the more recent, post-World War II migrants, called for an end to discrimination, marginalization, and economic disadvantage.

The government's Royal Commission on Bilingualism and Biculturalism, as the very name suggests, operated with an appreciation of the fact that the French minority occupied a special status in the nation, being considered along with the British one of the two "charter groups." Canada, for example, officially became a bilingual nation, with English and French being the dual languages of government. At the same time, the commission's members understood that there was a need to reckon with the fact that non-charter groups had legitimate grievances that needed to be addressed simultaneously with the demands of French-speaking Canada. To that end a Ministry of Multiculturalism was created in 1973 to monitor the imple- mentation of the following multicultural initiatives: assisting groups to maintain and foster their identities; assisting the same groups to overcome barriers to full incorporation into Canadian society, promoting opportunities for constructive engagements among groups, and assisting immigrants to become competent in one of the nation's two official languages.

Canada's embrace of multiculturalism become further insti- tutionalized with the passage of the Multiculturalism Act, which went into effect in 1988, making the nation the first in the world to implement an official state-sanctioned and -promoted policy of multiculturalism. With this law, programs were created to facilitate cross-cultural understanding, to maintain and strengthen the nation's different ethnic cultures, to promote them as part of a shared national heritage, and to support policies that allow people from all ethnic groups to participate fully in Canadian society.

CRITICS AND CHALLENGES

Canada's official multiculturalism is not without its critics. One such critic is Neil Bissoondath (2002), a Trinidad-born immigrant and writer who criticized what he called the "cult of multiculturalism" for encouraging ethnic groups to live in isolation from the larger society where their particularistic group identities are reinforced and strengthened, while the process of identifying with and embracing Canadian identity is impeded. He was not alone in this criticism. The idea that multiculturalism is divisive was echoed by other commentators. It was also a view that reflected public opinion. While the Canadian public is more supportive of multiculturalism than its counterparts in the other advanced industrial nations, it also has concerns about existing policy. Canadians appear relatively comfortable with the reality of Canada as a diverse society, but at the same time are anxious about the possibility that multiculturalism on the ground has promoted respect for difference without expending sufficient attention to the flip side of the coin, which is the need for all Canadians to see themselves as united with others on the basis of a shared citizenship.

As in other countries increasingly receptive to multiculturalism, Canada has been forced to wrestle with the competing demands of claims for recognition based on particularistic aspects of ethnic identity and countervailing claims based on more universal principles. This could be seen, for example, in the dispute that arose when Sikhs in the Royal Canadian Mounted Police argued for an exemption from wearing the traditional police hat because of the religious requirement that adult men wear a turban. The Sikhs and their supporters argued that an exemption was warranted as a mark of respect for a minority religion, while their opponents (which included a group of retired members of the force) contended that wearing a turban instead of the RCMP hat amounted to a violation of the organization's secular character (Parekh 2000: 244). In this particular case, the courts ultimately sided with the Sikhs, who were permitted to wear their turbans while on duty.

Are the critics right about the ethnic separatism created by multiculturalism? The evidence does not support such claims. For example, immigrants to Canada opt to become naturalized citizens at a higher rate than their counterparts in the US, which is not an official multicultural nation. Likewise, rates of residential segregation are lower in Canada than the US. Since multiculturalism became an official state policy, rates of intermarriage have increased rather than decreased. In short, not only does this evidence suggest that multiculturalism does not threaten to disunite the nation, but rather that many of the integrative outcomes look surprisingly like those in nations that subscribe to assimilation.

TRANSNATIONALISM AND CONTEMPORARY IMMIGRANTS

The difference between assimilation and multiculturalism revolves around the fact that the former seeks simply to integrate while the latter attempts to simultaneously integrate and achieve diversity. In this regard, transnationalism enters the picture, not as yet another mode of incorporation, but rather as a phenomenon that can tip the preferred mode of incorporation in the direction of multiculturalism. To understand why this is the case, we need first to describe what transnationalism means.

One of the hallmarks of the contemporary world is that globalization has led to the creation of a far more interrelated world than ever before. Globalization theorists have spent considerable energy spelling out the myriad ways that this interrelatedness has economic, political, cultural, and environmental implications. While transnationalism and globalization are not synonyms, they are connected concepts. Our concern here is with transnationalism and immigration.

We live, as some commentators have pointed out, in a world in motion. The United Nations recently reported that by the middle of the first decade of the current century there were nearly 200 million people living outside of the country where they were born. While this number constitutes a small percentage of the world's overall population, it also represents a twofold increase over the course of the past century.

One of the realities of the contemporary world is that it is far easier for immigrants to maintain contact with their point of origin than was the case in earlier periods, including the period of the last major migratory wave that began in the late nineteenth century and ended around the time of the Great Depression. Whereas a century ago immigrants had to rely on letters to maintain contacts with friends and family left behind, today it is possible for many to be in contact on a routine basis due to the availability of new communications technologies. The internet has played a significant role in this process, but perhaps more importantly is the telephone, especially since the advent of cheap phone cards. Likewise, improvements in travel technologies have made movement back and forth between place of origin and point of destination considerably easier. While immigrants in an earlier era had to rely on arduous journeys by steamship and train, today's immigrants make extensive use of air travel. Newcomers to the US once arrived at Ellis Island by ship. Today they land at JFK International Airport.

The net result, according to those who have studied transnationalism practices, is that a unique social field is often created that transcends political boundaries, a social space in which patterns of interaction arise that link the immigrants to those that stay behind. This situation is depicted in Figure 5.2. The result is that immigrants are more likely to preserve aspects of their ethnic identity than otherwise might have

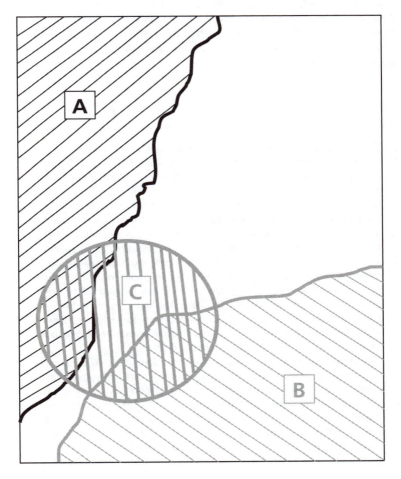

Figure 5.2: Transnational social spaces.

been the case, while at the same time those who have remained in the homeland are influenced by their émigré counterparts who bring with them new ideas and ways of living from their new country. The core group that makes such a field possible are the individuals who move back and forth between two localities with a certain regularity, living, in effect, with one foot in both places. These individuals are bilingual and have an economic, and sometimes a political, stake in both homeland and destination (Portes, *et al.* 1999: 217). Box 5.3 offers two concrete examples from the work of sociological ethnographers on transnational communities, one with immigrants from the Dominican Republic residing in Boston and the other from Mexican immigrants living in New York City.

Box 5.3 Two examples of transnationalism.

Transnationalism does not only involve those who move to and fro. It also impacts those around them in both localities. In Robert C. Smith's (2006) study of Mexican immigrants in New York City from the same town of Ticuani, a hometown association established in Brooklyn worked with those who remained in Mexico to improve the community's infrastructure, which included creating a potable water system, paving and lighting the town square, building a primary and secondary school, and renovating a church damaged by an earthquake. This aspect of transnationalism links remittances—the sending of money and goods to people remaining behind—to economic development. The Mexican government has seen this potential and has attempted to both stimulate and control such capital flows by instituting what became known as the 3 × 1 Program, which provides three dollars (from federal, state, and local governments) for each dollar donated by hometown associations for government-approved projects.

Another example of transnationalism that illustrates cultural transfers rather than economic ones can be seen in Peggy Levitt's study of Dominican immigrants from Mirafloreños living in the Jamaica Plain neighborhood of Boston. In part of her study, religious change brought about by immigration is analyzed (Levitt 2001: 159–179). The Roman Catholic Church hierarchy in Boston did not opt to create distinctly Dominican congregations, but instead offered them pan-Latino churches composed of immigrants from Central America,

South America, and the Caribbean. One of the results of this practice was that those religious practices and attitudes that were distinctly Dominican had to give way to what Levitt (2001: 169) calls a "least-common-denominator Catholicism." While assimilation theory would have predicted such accommodation to a new environment, what the transnational perspective adds to the picture is the impact of such a transformation on those who remained behind in the Dominican Republic. The ongoing communication between family members in Mirafloreños and Boston, the role of remittances, and the impact of Dominican priests trained in the US led to changes in the way people in the homeland viewed and practiced their religious faith.

HOW MANY TRANSNATIONAL IMMIGRANTS?

One question that has frequently been raised concerns the number of transnational immigrants. The most rigorous research projects to date that have explored this question have concluded that only a relatively small percentage of immigrants are transnational (Levitt and Jaworsky 2007). Nonetheless, it may only take a relatively small number of transnational migrants to create a transnational social space that involves those who stayed behind and those who moved but do not continue to move back and forth between the homeland and host society. In other words, the relatively small number may lead to the misleading conclusion that the extent to which economic, political, and cultural transnationalism is occurring has been overestimated. Portes (2003: 877) makes this case when he writes, "Despite its limited numerical character, the combination of a cadre of regular transnational activists with the occasional activities of other migrants adds up to a social process of significant economic and social impact for communities and even nations." The bottom line is that at the moment there is abundant evidence to suggest that transnationalism is a significant phenomenon. Insofar as this is the case, it serves as a stimulus for multiculturalism rather than assimilationism as the mode of incorporation preferred by immigrants.

The unanswered question is whether transnationalism will continue into the future. Will people who are at present involved in transnational networks continue to be involved over the course of their lives? Will, for example, the Ticuani immigrants in New York City that we discussed above continue to work on public works projects in their hometown, or might their energies be directed to improving living condition in their New York City neighborhood? Of course, such pursuits are not mutually exclusive: people can simultaneously be involved in such activities in both the homeland and receiving country. However, Smith discovered in his study that those active in the homeland were not very invested in political and social life in the receiving society.

BEYOND THE FIRST GENERATION

A more significant question is whether transnationalism is a phenomenon limited to the first generation. Will the children of immigrants be as invested in transnationalism as their parents were? What about the third generation and beyond? We can only speculate about what the future holds, but research has recently begun on the second generation. Albeit limited, the research to date would appear to indicate that with generational succession we can expect a decline in transnational practices. However, the historical record suggests that it is far too early to conclude that transnationalism is destined to fade away. The continuing interest of some groups, including Jews in the US, in homeland politics is an indication that transnationalism may prove to be durable.

REGIONAL AUTONOMY AND INCORPORATION

Ethnonational minorities pose a different sort of incorporative issue. Unlike immigrants, who tend to assume that they need at some level to adapt and adjust to the culture of the receiving nation, ethnonational minorities have a long history within that geographic locale and assume that they have a right to survive as a group rather than acculturate into the larger society. Their identity is defined in part because of territorial claims they make. The case of the francophone community in Canada's province of Quebec was mentioned earlier. Parallel to Quebec are other ethnonational regions in the world's liberal democracies include Scotland, Wales, and Northern Ireland in the United Kingdom and the Basque region and Catalonia in Spain.

In all of these examples, some nationalist activists have defined their ethnonational group as a stateless nation and have demanded independence. In two cases—Northern Ireland and the Basque—militant organizations have for the past few decades engaged in campaigns of violence.

The three other ethnonationalist movements have largely repudiated violence, pursuing their political goals with ballots, not bullets. They have organized political parties to advance their objectives. This would not be possible in a repressive political climate. Indeed, in Spain it was not possible during the long repressive Franco dictatorship, during which time Catalonian and Basque nationalism were forced underground as the regime implemented policies aimed at destroying their cultures and languages. Though not as repressive, the Thatcher years in the UK were ones in which the government did little to accommodate the political aspirations of its ethnonational minorities.

REGIONAL AUTONOMY

Existing nation-states are in general unwilling to allow their current boundaries to be reduced in size due to the withdrawal of one of its regions. Seeking to prevent such a situation from occurring can be contained by force, but this generally leads to increased levels of societal tension and conflict. As an alternative to repression, which does not advance the incorporation of minorities, nation-states have at their disposal a mechanism that accommodates ethnonational minorities while simultaneously preserving their territorial integrity. The mechanism in question is the granting of regional autonomy.

This is precisely what the administration of Tony Blair did in the UK when it implemented a policy known as **devolution**. What it meant was that Scotland and Wales were given considerable control over domestic policies in their respective regions. They were granted the ability to set policies regarding education, transportation, commerce, and so forth rather than having those policies dictated by the nation's central parliament in London. At the same time, foreign policy is determined solely by the central government. Scotland opened its own parliament, while in Wales a counterpart assembly was created. Residents both elected members to parliament in nationwide elections and they elected members to represent them in these two regional chambers.

Why would the New Labour government launched by Tony Blair push such a policy? In part, in accordance with the dictates of multiculturalism, it was prepared to concede both Scotland and Wales had their own cultural histories separate from that of England, and to agree that residents in each locale had a right to try to preserve their cultures. Related to this, both regions were poorer than the nation as a whole, and were considerably poorer than the southeast of England. Thus, part of their increased ability to set economic policies for their region was based on recognition of the fact that both Scotland and Wales had historically lacked control over their economic destinies and this had put them over time at a distinct disadvantage. In short, devolution could be seen as a policy designed to promote both recognition or respect and redistribution.

PREVENTING ETHNIC SEPARATISM

However, there was also an element of self-interest on the part of the nation-state. The UK, after all, did not want the nation to be dismantled as a result of successful campaigns on the part of ethnonationalist movements aimed at achieving independence. As early as the 1970s, commentator Tom Nairn (1977) predicted the "break-up of Britain." A little more than two decades later, he would write about life "after Britain" (Nairn 2000). The claim that Britain has somehow ceased to exist obviously has an element of hyperbole to it, but it is based on the assumption that the process of granting greater autonomy to the regions is a stepping stone on the way to independence. This is clearly what the leadership of the Scottish Nationalist Party thinks, too. However, the reason that the government implemented devolution was that it thought that granting regional autonomy would defuse the separatist threat insofar as it would be seen by a majority of people in Scotland and Wales as a sufficient response to their demands. As such, the policy represents something of a gamble, and it is difficult to predict what the future portends. However, at the moment there is little likelihood that Scotland will soon become an independent nation, while the chances that this will occur in Wales appear to be even more remote.

This approach to the challenges that ethnonationalist movements pose to nation states has not been confined to the UK. One sees it as well in Spain, where people in both Catalonia and the Basque region have achieved greater say over their lives. It can be seen, not only with ethnonational minorities, but with indigenous peoples as well.

CONCLUSION

As this chapter indicates, there are two main ways—or modes of incorporation—that ethnic minorities that have experienced social exclusion come to become a part of a society's mainstream: assimilation and multiculturalism. Transnationalism, which amounts to immigrants seeking to live with one foot in the homeland and one in the receiving nation, serves to reinforce multiculturalism at the expense of assimilation. For ethnonational minorities and indigenous peoples, policies granting regional autonomy also serve to promote multiculturalism. Thus, it is not surprising that, despite the controversy that surrounds it, multiculturalism ought to be seen as a novel form of societal inclusion that is unlikely to be repudiated.

EPILOGUE

During the formative period of sociology, many of the most influential social thinkers of their era thought that divisions based on ethnic attachments—which, as we have stressed throughout this book includes racialized ethnicity, ethnonationalism, and religio-ethnicity— would progressively erode and disappear. One version of this sort of thinking shaped Marxist thought, which was predicated on the assumption that the most fundamental divisions in society were class based. Ethnicity was sometimes a complicating factor that needed to be considered, but in the end one of the remarkable things about capitalism was that it would act like a solvent to dissolve ethnic divisions, thereby exposing in the starkest of ways the fact that class divisions in capitalism were the root cause of inequality. Class divisions were the source of the exploitation and alienation inevitably produced by capitalism. As workers gained consciousness of this reality, as they became class conscious, ethnic and other forms of solidarity and division would fade in significance.

From another perspective, that of what became known broadly as modernization theory, there was an underlying assumption that ethnicity would progressively erode and become an inconsequential feature of social life. Rather than a society based on deep emotional attachments to those who were presumed to have ties of blood, history, and tradition—or in other words, a society based on a shared commitment to remaining connected to the past—modernization theorists predicted a future in which individuals would free themselves from old, ascriptive bonds and would orient their worldviews to the future. In the modern world based on individual achievement and rationality, ethnicity would come to be viewed as an artifact of a world rooted in tradition, its salience eroding with the passage of time.

As sociology came into its own after this formative period, those scholars who devoted their energies to studying ethnicity in its many guises came to realize that the ethnic factor in social life was not going to disappear anytime soon. In fact, many concluded that ethnic affiliations and ethnic relations would remain obdurate features of the modern world long into the foreseeable future. Some went so far as to reconsider a position that the mainstream of the discipline had earlier rejected, namely that ethnicity was somehow a primordial characteristic of human beings. In other words, so it was claimed, ethnicity was in effect hardwired into the psyches of all humans. As such, ethnic groups have in the past and would continue in the future to seek to advance their own collective self interests and when those interests got in the way of other groups doing likewise, conflict would inevitably occur. Such, in effect, is the way of the world. In other words, whereas both Marxist and modernization theorists predicted the gradual fading away of the ethnic factor in contemporary social life, the primordialists contended that the more things change, the more they stay the same. Ethnicity was in the past, is at present, and can be expected to be in the future both a powerful source of identity and collective solidarity and the underlying source of ethnic conflict.

The purpose of this book is to equip students with a sociological perspective on ethnicity that we believe steers a course between these two positions—a course that we think has been laid out by a substantial body of sociological research and theorizing over the course of more than a century. The scholars who have contributed to staking out that course have offered a rather wide range of perspectives on the topic, which is evident in our summary overview of that work. Nevertheless, we think that some basic lessons can be distilled from this work that few among the ranks of race and ethnic relations scholars would disagree with.

First, ethnicity and ethnic relations are social constructions. This means that they are the product of collectivities acting in concert and interacting with other collectivities in the context of existing social, cultural, and political settings. As such, they are subject to change when social actors act in ways that promote change, while they remain fixed and permanent-looking when social actors act in ways that promote the status quo. By stressing the constructed character of ethnicity, we seek to avoid the problems associated with viewing ethnic groups as givens rather than as ongoing achievements, the result of interactions that are sustained over time.

Second, ethnicity is often a source of community, creating solidarity among group members. When an ethnic culture exists that provides its members with a sense of meaning and purpose, offering a compelling way of life, it can have a profound impact on members' sense of self. It connects people to their pasts while providing the basis for maintaining present-day social relationships. When this occurs, not only is the culture in question seen to be worth preserving and embracing, but an institutional presence arises to help ensure that this happens. We don't want to romanticize ethnicity, however, for while some might see it as a source of solidarity and meaning, others view it as unduly restricting, with a culture they cannot or will not embrace. Some ethnic cultures work against the interests of women. Some promote values that are undemocratic and illiberal. Not surprisingly, in such instances, many people either want to see the ethnic culture change or they want to leave the group. What this means, quite simply, is that just as ethnicity can promote intra-group solidarity, so it can also be a source of intra-group tension. Whereas some people will remain loyal members of an ethnic group, others will seek to exit.

Third, much of the focus of this book has been on interethnic, rather than intra-ethnic relations. The chapters of this book reflect those topics that have received the most sustained attention by the sociological community. Much of that attention focuses on the dark side of ethnic relations, including studies devoted to analyzing the causes and consequences of prejudice, discrimination, inequality, and conflict. As is evident in the respective chapters that address these topics, all exist in highly variable and complex ways, predicated on the interplay between larger, structured patterns of interaction and the particularities of specific places at specific historical moments.

The variability and complexity of these phenomena make the sorts of broader conceptual generalizations sociologists aim for especially challenging. This is evident throughout the preceding chapters, but perhaps nowhere so clearly than in the survey of competing models for accounting for prejudice. That there is no general consensus about how best to study any of these topics, with various theoretical perspectives competing with other perspectives, is a reflection of the difficulties associated with understanding "ties of blood" that bind people to collectivities and often pit them against other collectivities defined by different blood ties. Ethnicity in all its guises needs to be analyzed both in terms of the rational features of ethnic affiliations and interethnic relations, but also in terms of the emotions that often play a powerful role in shaping those affiliations and relations. In trying to make sense of it all, sociologists have their work cut out for them. But we think that contemporary sociologists benefit by being able to build on a long tradition of research and theorizing, and that they have an important role to play in the future as they use their tools of analysis to make sense of the ethnic factor in contemporary social life.

Finally, the sociology of ethnicity has a role to play in informing public discourse on ethnic relations. The societies most readers of this book live in are more, not less, diverse than they were in the past. Moreover, as globalization links people from different nations, learning to live with those who are different—be it physically, culturally, linguistically, religiously, or some combination thereof—or, in other words, learning to live with diversity takes on an added dimension, and an added urgency. The challenges ahead revolve around learning to live together in relative harmony, respecting people and cultures different from one's own, while at the same time promoting social justice by seeking to overcome inequality and marginalization based on ethnic origin. Or to put it slightly differently, the challenge for people of good will is to find positive ways to recognize the other, while insuring that valued resources are distributed equitably to all people regardless of ethnic background. The starting point for addressing this challenge is recognition of the fact that in spite of diversity, we share a common humanity.

GLOSSARY

annexation the incorporation of territory into an existing political unit such as a nation

assimilation the process of incorporating minority groups into the culture and social institutions of the dominant society that stresses an overarching common shared identity

color-blind policies a term used to describe policies that are formulated by disregarding racial considerations, seen, for example, in efforts to eliminate affirmative action plans in college admissions and in employment practices

cultural pluralism a situation where diverse groups live in harmony with other groups while maintaining a degree of separate collective identities

devolution a British policy of granting greater regional autonomy to Scotland, Wales, and Northern Ireland

discrimination actions that have a negative impact on the life circumstances and chances of individuals or groups

essentialize to treat race or ethnicity (or other ascribed identities such as gender or sexual orientation) as fixed and unchanging, which is typically explained as the consequence of biological factors rather than social or cultural ones

ethnic cleansing a term that arose during the Balkan conflicts of the 1990s to refer to campaigns of removing or eliminating members of a particular ethnic group from a territory through acts of genocide or forced removal—or both

ethnicity a form of collective identity based on a subjective belief in a shared culture—which can include a shared language, religion, values, and practices—and a common history

ethnie a synonym for "ethnic group"

ethnocentrism negative assessments of other groups that use the in-group as the standard of that which is good, right, just, beautiful, and so forth, with out-groups that are most different from the in-group being viewed in the most negative light

ethnonational minority an ethnic group within a larger nation-state that considers itself to be a nation, with a shared language, culture, and territorial concentration

Eugenics a program aimed at improving the human race through policies to control populations selectively through hereditary means

genocide the intentional and organized murder of the whole or part of an ethnic group (including national, racial, and religious groups)

human capital the education, training, and other skills and knowledge—along with the credentials that legitimate them—that define the productive potential of an individual

hypersegregation a term coined by Douglas Massey and Nancy Denton to describe high levels of residential segregation and offering a new way to measure segregation that is intended to remedy the shortcomings of alternative methods

hypodescent the process of assigning children of mixed unions to membership in the less privileged of the two groups

income the wages an individual earns through gainful employment

indigenous people an ethnic group that has the earliest historical connection to a geographic region

irredentism an attempt by a state to incorporate territory inhabited by members of the state's dominant ethnic group, or of ethnics outside of a state to connect with their ethnic counterparts in the state

Jim Crow racism the policies enacted in the American South after the Civil War to ensure the subordination and segregation of African Americans, policies backed up by the use of both legal and extra-legal violence

laissez-faire racism a contemporary form of racism that actively opposes policy initiatives aimed at addressing racial inequalities, instead explaining such differences in terms of cultural explanations for the existing racial stratification order

mestizo an interracial individual who is the offspring of a white European-origin parent and an indigenous parent

mulatto an interracial individual who is the offspring of a white European-origin parent and a black African-origin parent

multiculturalism a mode of incorporating minority groups into the larger society that allows for the maintenance of cultural diversity

nationalism an ideology that defines a people as constituting a political community on the basis of such features as shared ethnicity, language, or religion or on the basis of a shared commitment to certain civic values

panethnic a collective identity resulting from the grouping of two or more distinct ethnic groups, as when the term Asian is used in reference to Chinese, Japanese, Korean, Vietnamese, and other groups from Southeast Asia

prejudice negative attitudes directed at individuals of groups on account of their membership in those groups

race a grouping or classification of people based on what are presumed to be biological differences typically evident as differences in physical appearance due to such features as skin color

race relations cycle a theory of the evolution of relations between ethnic groups moving from contact to conflict to accommodation, finally arriving at assimilation

racial formation a theory that views racial orders as an unstable, often durable, but nonetheless historically specific result of the interaction between state and interest group actors operating in a particular ideological field

racialized ethnicity an ethnic identity in which the racial dimension acquires particular significance

redlining the practice of denying mortgage loans and property insurance to residents of inner-city poor neighborhoods with high concentrations of minority residents

segmented assimilation a theory that contends immigrants may assimilate in three directions: into the mainstream, downward into the lower class, or by remaining attached to the ethnic enclave

Social Darwinism a nineteenth century attempt to apply evolutionary thought to society, premised on the assumption that social evolution operated like a natural law and that its key characteristic was that the strongest, those fit for survival, would eventually thrive while the weak perished

social capital the relationships a person has with others, often based on family origins, that provides access to valuable benefits and resources

social distance scale a measurement of the perceived distance between groups as defined by group members, and thus a measure of prejudice

social dominance theory a psychological theory predicated on the assumption that all human societies are defined in hierarchal terms that seeks to account for how such hierarchies are created and preserved over time

subtle racism in contrast to traditional racism, this manifestation of racism is directed against out-groups in general, rather than directed at specific targets, and expresses itself covertly, often through the use of code words

symbolic ethnicity a term coined by Herbert Gans to describe a situation where people maintain an emotional attachment to an ethnic identity without the attachment requiring behavioral consequences or, in other words, where people want to feel ethnic

symbolic racism a form of racism in which anti-black feelings are attached to the belief that blacks violate and are hostile to core American values

transnationalism immigrant activities leading to the creation of social fields that permit them to establish themselves in the receiving nation while maintaining ties—political, economic, and cultural—with the homeland

wealth the sum total of the valued resources an individual possesses, including property, stocks, bonds, savings, and retirement annuities

white privilege a perspective that examines both the benefits that accrue to being white and the varied ways that most whites account for their success vis-à-vis less successful minority groups

REFERENCES

Adorno, Theodor, Else Frenkel-Brunswik, Daniel J. Levinson, and R. Nevitt Sanford. 1950. *The Authoritarian Personality*. New York: John Wiley and Sons.

Alaimo, Katherine, Ronnette R. Briefel, Edward A. Frongillo, Jr., and Christine M. Olson. 1998. "Food Insufficiency Exists in the United States: Results from the Third National Health and Nutrition Examination Survey (NHANES III). *American Journal of Public Health*, 88(5): 419–426.

Alba, Richard. 1990. *Ethnic Identity: The Transformation of White America*. New Haven, CT: Yale University Press.

Alba, Richard. 2010. "Connecting the Dots between Boundary Change and Large-Scale Assimilation with Zolbergian Clues." *Social Research*, 77(1): 163–180.

Alba, Richard D., John R. Logan, and Paul E. Bellair. 1994. "Living with Crime: The Implications of Racial/Ethnic Differences in Suburban Location." *Social Forces*, 73(3): 395–434.

Alexander, Jeffrey C. 2006. *The Civil Sphere*. New York: Oxford University Press.

Allport, Gordon W. 1954. *The Nature of Prejudice*. Cambridge, MA: Addison-Wesley.

Anderson, Elijah. 2000. *Code of the Street: Decency, Violence, and the Moral Life of the Inner City*. New York: W. W. Norton.

Athanias, Floya. 1992. "Connecting 'Race' and Ethnic Phenomena." *Sociology*, 26(3): 421–438.

Baldassare, Mark, ed. 1994. *The Los Angeles Riots: Lessons for the Urban Future*. Boulder, CO: Westview Press.

Bales, Kevin. 1999. *Disposable People: New Slavery in the Global Economy*. Berkeley, CA: University of California Press.

Banton, Michael. 1987. *Racial Theories*. Cambridge: Cambridge University Press.

Barrett, James R. and David Roediger. 1997. "In-between Peoples: Race, Nationality, and the 'New Immigrant' Working Class." *Journal of American Ethnic History*, 16(3): 3–44.

Bastin, Rohan. 2009. "Sri Lankan Civil Society and Its Fanatics." *Social Analysis*, 53(1): 123–140.

Bauman, Zygmunt. 1992. *Mortality, Immortality, and Other Life Strategies*. Stanford, CA: Stanford University Press.

Berger, Ronald J. 2002. *Fathoming the Holocaust: A Social Problems Approach*. New York: Aldine de Gruyter.

Bhattacharya, Jayanta, Thomas Deleire, Steven Haider, and Janet Currie. 2002. "Heat or Eat? Cold Weather Shocks and Nutrition in Poor American Families." National Bureau of Economic Research Working Paper No. W9004.

Bissoondath, Neil. 2002. *Selling Illusions: The Cult of Multiculturalism in Canada*. Toronto: Penguin.

Blalock, Hubert M. 1967. *Toward a Theory of Minority-Group Relations*. New York: John Wiley and Sons.

Blumer, Herbert. 1958. "Race Prejudice as a Sense of Group Position." *The Pacific Sociological Review*, 1(1): 3–7.

Bobo, Lawrence and Ryan Smith. 1998. "From Jim Crow Racism to Laissez-Faire Racism: The Transformation of Racial Attitudes." In Wendy Katkin, Ned Landsman, and Andrea Tyree, eds., *Beyond Pluralism: The Concept of Group and Group Identity in America*. Urbana, IL: University of Illinois Press, pp. 182–220.

Bogardus, Emory. 1933. "A Social Distance Scale." *Sociology and Social Research*, 17(January-February): 265–271.

Bonilla-Silva, Eduardo. 2001. *White Supremacy and Racism in the Post-Civil Rights Era*. Boulder, CO: Lynne Rienner.

Bonilla-Silva, Eduardo. 2010. *Racism without Racists: Color-Blind Racism and the Persistence of Racial Inequality in the United States*, third edition. Lanham, MD: Rowman & Littlefield.

Bonilla-Silva, Eduardo and Tyrone Forman. 2000. "I Am Not Racist, but …: Mapping White College Students' Racial Ideology in the USA." *Discourse and Society*, 11(1): 50–85.

Boyd, Monica. 2002. "Educational Attainment of Immigrant Offspring: Success or Segmented Assimilation?" *International Migration Review*, 36(4): 1037–1060.

Brown, Rupert. 1995. *Prejudice: Its Social Psychology*. Oxford: Blackwell.

Brubaker, Rogers. 2004. *Ethnicity without Groups*. Cambridge, MA: Harvard University Press.

Bureau of Justice Statistics. 2002. *Homicide Trends in the U.S.: Trends by Race*. Formerly available online at: www.ojp.usdoj.gov/bjs/homicide/race.htm.

Bureau of Justice Statistics. 2003. *Victim Characteristics: Annual Household Income*. Formerly available online at: www.ojp.usdoj.gov/bjs/cvict_v.htm.

Carmichael, Stokley and Charles V. Hamilton. 1967. *Black Power: The Politics of Liberation in America*. New York: Random House.

Chicago Commission on Race Relations. 1922. *The Negro in Chicago: A Study of Race Relations and a Race Riot*. Chicago, IL: University of Chicago Press.

Chung, Chanjin and Samuel L. Myers, Jr. 1999. "Do the Poor Pay More for Food? An Analysis of Grocery Store Availability and Food Price Disparities." *The Journal of Consumer Affairs*, 33(3): 276–296.

Collins, Randall. 1975. *Conflict Sociology: Toward an Explanatory Science*. New York: Academic Press.

Connor, Walker. 1994. *Ethnonationalism: The Quest for Understanding*. Princeton, NJ: Princeton University Press.

Cornell, Stephen and Douglas Hartmann. 2007. *Ethnicity and Race: Making Identities in a Changing World*. Thousand Oaks, CA: Pine Forge Press.

Costanzo, Mark. 1997. *Just Revenge: Costs and Consequences of the Death Penalty*. New York: St. Martin's Press.

Crul, Maurice and Jens Schneider. 2010. "Comparative Integration Context Theory: Participation and Belonging in New Diverse European Cities." *Ethnic and Racial Studies*, 33(7): 1249–1268).

Dadrian, Vahakn N. 1989. "Genocide as a Problem of National and International Law: The World War I Armenian Case and Its Contemporary Legal Ramifications." *Yale Journal of International Law*, 14(2): 221–334.

Davis, Kingsley and Wilbert E. Moore. 1944. "Some Principles of Stratification." *American Sociological Review*, 10(2): 242–249.

DeNavas-Walt, Carmen, Bernadette D. Proctor, and Robert J. Mills. 2004. *Income, Poverty, and Health Insurance Coverage in the United States: 2003*. US Census Bureau, Current Population Reports, P60–226. Washington DC: US Government Printing Office.

Dollard, John. 1937. *Caste and Class in a Southern Town*. New Haven, CT: Yale University Press.

Domhoff, William. 2011. "Wealth, Income, and Power." Online, available at: http://sociology.ucsc.edu/whorulesamerica/power/wealth.html.

Duster, Troy. 2003. *Backdoor to Eugenics*, second edition. London: Routledge.

Duster, Troy. 2006. "The Molecular Reinscription of Race: Unanticipated Issues in Biotechnology and Forensic Science." *Patterns of Prejudice*, 40(4/5): 427–441.

Esman, Milton. 2004. *An Introduction to Ethnic Conflict*. Malden, MA: Blackwell.

Evans, Gary W. and Elyse Kantrowitz. 2002. "Socioeconomic Status and Health: The Potential Role of Environmental Risk Exposure." *Annual Review of Public Health*, 23: 303–331.

Evans, J. A. S. 1996. "The Present State of Canada." *The Virginia Quarterly*, 72(3): 213–225.

Feagin, Joe. 2001. *Racist America: Roots, Current Realities, and Future Reparations*. New York: Routledge.

Feagin, Joe. 2006. *Systemic Racism: A Theory of Oppression*. New York: Routledge.

Fenton, Steve. 1999. *Ethnicity: Racism, Class, and Culture*. London: Macmillan.

Fischer, Claude S., Michael Hout, Martin Sanchez Jankowski, and Samuel R. Lucas, eds. 1996. *Inequality by Design: Cracking the Bell Curve Myth*. Princeton, NJ: Princeton University Press.

Frank, Robert H. and Philip J. Cook. 1995. *The Winner-Take-All Society*. New York: The Free Press.

Frankenberg, Ruth. 1994. *White Racism, Race Matters: The Social Construction of Whiteness*. New York: Routledge.

Fredrickson, George M. 2002. *Racism: A Short History*. Princeton, NJ: Princeton University Press.

Fredrickson, George M. 2008. *Diverse Nations: Explorations in the History of Racial and Ethnic Pluralism*. Boulder, CO: Paradigm.

Gaertner, Samuel L. and John F. Dovidio. 1986. "The Aversive Form of Racism." In John F. Dovidio and Samuel L. Gaertner, eds., *Prejudice, Discrimination, and Racism*. Orlando, FL: Academic Press, pp. 71–89.

Gans, Herbert. 1979. "Symbolic Ethnicity: The Future of Ethnic Groups and Cultures in America." *Ethnic and Racial Studies*, 2(1): 1–20.

Gans, Herbert. 1999. *Making Sense of America: Sociological Analyses and Essays*. Lanham, MD: Rowman & Littlefield.

Geronimus, Arline T., John Bound, Timothy A. Waidmann, Cynthia G. Colen, and Dianne Steffick. 2001. "Inequality in Life Expectancy, Functional Status, and Active Life Expectancy across Selected Black and White Populations in the United States." *Demography*, 38(3): 227–251.

Gilroy, Paul. 2000. *Against Race: Imagining Political Culture beyond the Color Line*. Cambridge, MA: The Belknap Press of Harvard University Press.

Gitlin, Todd, 1995. *The Twilight of Common Dreams: Why American Is Wracked by Culture Wars*. New York: Metropolitan Books.

Glazer, Nathan. 1997. *We Are All Multiculturalists Now*. Cambridge, MA: Harvard University Press.

Gobineau, Comte Arthur de. 1915 [1853–1855]. *The Inequality of Human Races*. London: Heinemann.

Goffman, Erving. 1961. *Asylums: Essays on the Social Situation of Mental Patients and Other Inmates*. Garden City, NY: Doubleday & Company.

Goldhagen, Daniel. 1996. *Hitler's Willing Executioners: Ordinary Germans and the Holocaust*. New York: Alfred A. Knopf.

Gordon, Milton M. 1964. *Assimilation in American Life: The Role of Race, Religion, and National Origins*. New York: Oxford University Press.

Gourevitch, Philip. 1998. *We Wish to Inform You That Tomorrow We Will Be Killed with Our Families: Stories from Rwanda*. New York: Farrar, Straus, and Giroux.

Greeley, Andrew. 1974. *Ethnicity in the United States: A Preliminary Reconnaissance*. New York: John Wiley & Sons.

Guibernau, Montserrat. 1999. *Nations without States: Political Communities in a Global Age*. Cambridge: Polity.

Hacker, Jacob S. and Paul Pierson. 2010. "Winner-Take-All Politics: Public Policy, Political Organization, and the Precipitous Rise of Top Incomes in the United States." *Politics and Society*, 38(2): 152–204.

Herrnstein, Richard J. and Charles Murray. 1994. *The Bell Curve: Intelligence and Class Structure in American Life*. New York: Free Press.

Hilberg, Raul. 2003. *The Destruction of the European Jews*, three vols., third edition. New Haven, CT: Yale University Press.

Hoffman, Kathryn, Charmaine Llagas, and Thomas D. Snyder. 2003. *Status and Trends in the Education of Blacks*. (Report No. NCES-2003-034). Washington, DC: National Center for Education Statistics. (ERIC Document Reproduction Service No. ED481811).

Horowitz, Donald. 1985. *Ethnic Groups in Conflict*. Berkeley, CA: University of California Press.

Horowitz, Donald. 2001. *The Deadly Ethnic Riot*. Berkeley, CA: University of California Press.

Hughes, C. Everett. 1971[1948]. *The Sociological Eye: Selected Papers*. Chicago, IL: Aldine-Atherton.

Hughes, Michael and Melvin E. Thomas. 1998. "The Continuing Significance of Race Revisited: A Study of Race, Class, and Quality of Life in America, 1972–1996. *American Sociological Review*, 63(4): 785–795.

Human Rights Watch. 2002. *Race and Incarceration in the United States*, Human Rights Watch Backgrounder, February 27. Online, available at: www.hrw.org/legacy/backgrounder/usa/race/.

Huntington, Samuel. 2004. *Who Are We? The Challenges to America's National Identity*. New York: Simon & Schuster.

Iceland, John. 2009. *Where We Now Live: Immigration and Race in the United States*. Berkeley, CA: University of California Press.

Ignatiev, Noel. 1995. *How the Irish Became White*. London: Routledge.

Jacobs, Jerry. 1996. "Gender Inequality and Higher Education." *Annual Review of Sociology*, 22: 153–185.

Ivison, Duncan. 2010. "Introduction: Multiculturalism as a Public Ideal." In Duncan Ivison, ed., *The Ashgate Research Companion to Multiculturalism*. Farnham: Ashgate, pp. 1–16.

Jacobson, Matthew Frye. 1998. *Whiteness of a Different Color: European Immigrants and the Alchemy of Race*. Cambridge, MA: Harvard University Press.

Jones, Arthur F. and Daniel H. Weinberg. 2000. *The Changing Shape of the Nation's Income Distribution*. US Census Bureau, Current Population Reports, P60–204. Washington DC: US Government Printing Office.

Kasinitz, Phillip, John. H. Mollenkopf, Mary C. Waters, and Jennifer Holdaway. 2008. *Inheriting the City: The Children of Immigrants Come of Age*. Cambridge, MA: and New York: Harvard University Press and Russell Sage Foundation.

Kaufman, Jason. 2007. "Sacralizing Separatism." *Sociological Forum*, 22(4): 584–587.

Kinder, Donald R. and Lynn M. Sanders. 1996. *Divided by Color: Racial Politics and Democratic Ideals*. Chicago, IL: University of Chicago Press.

Kinder, Donald R. and David Sears. 1981. "Prejudice and Politics: Symbolic Racism Versus Racial Threats to the Good Life." *Journal of Personality and Social Psychology*, 40(3): 414–431.

King, Russell (with Richard Black, Michael Collyer, Anthony Fielding, and Ronald Skeldon). 2010. *The Atlas of Human Migration: Global Patterns of People on the Move*. London: Earthscan.

Kivisto, Peter. 2004. "What is the Canonical Theory of Assimilation? Robert E. Park and His Predecessors." *Journal of the History of the Behavioral Sciences*, 40(2):1–15.

Kivisto, Peter. 2007. "Rethinking the Relationship between Ethnicity and Religion." In James Beckford and Jay Demerath, eds., *Handbook of the Sociology of Religion*. Thousand Oaks, CA: Sage, pp. 490–510.

Kivisto, Peter and Thomas Faist. 2010. *Beyond a Border: The Causes and Consequences of Contemporary Immigration*. Thousand Oaks, CA: Pine Forge/Sage.

Kluegel, James R. and Eliot R. Smith. 1986. *Beliefs about Inequality: Americans' Views of What Is and Ought to Be*. New York: Aldine de Gruyter.

Kymlicka, Will. 2005. *Multicultural Citizenship: A Liberal Theory of Minority Rights*. New York: Oxford University Press.

Lamont, Michele and Virag Molnar. 2002. "The Study of Boundaries in the Social Sciences." *Annual Review of Sociology*, 28: 167–195.

Laslett, Barbara. 2000. "The Poverty of (Monocausal) Theory: A Comment on Charles Tilly's *Durable Inequality*." *Comparative Studies in Society and History*, 42(2): 475–481.

Lee, Sandra Soo-Jin. 2005. "Racializing Drug Design: Implications of Pharmacogenomics for Health Disparities." *American Journal of Public Health,* 95(12): 2133–2138.

Levitt, Peggy and B. Nadya Jaworsky. 2007. "Transnational Migration Studies: Past Developments and Future Trends." *Annual Review of Sociology*, 33: 129–156.

Lin, Nan. 2000. Inequality in Social Capital. *Contemporary Sociology*, 29(6): 785–795.

Lipset, Seymour Martin. 1960. *Political Man: The Social Bases of Politics*. Garden City, NY: Doubleday & Company.

Lyman, Stanford. 1972. *The Black in American Sociological Thought: A Failure of Perspective*. New York: Capricorn Books.

Lyman, Stanford. 1992. *Militarism, Imperialism, and Racial Accommodation: An Analysis and Interpretation of the Early Writings of Robert E. Park*. Fayetteville, AR: University of Arkansas Press.

Marshall, Ray. 2000. *Back to Shared Prosperity: The Growing Inequality of Wealth and Income in America*. Armonk, NY: M. E. Sharpe.

Mason, David, 2000. *Race and Ethnicity in Modern Britain*, second edition. Oxford: Oxford University Press.

Massey, Douglas S. 2006. "Race, Class, and Markets: Social Policy in the 21st Century." In David B. Grusky and Ravi Kanbur, eds., *Poverty and Inequality*. Stanford, CA: Stanford University Press, pp. 117–132.

Massey, Douglas S. and Nancy Denton. 1993. *American Apartheid: Segregation and the Making of the Underclass*. Cambridge, MA: Harvard University Press.

Massey, Douglas S. and Eric Fong. 1990. "Segregation and Neighborhood Quality: Blacks, Hispanics, and Asians in the San Francisco Metropolitan Area." *Social Forces*, 69(1): 15–32.

McClintock, Anne. 1995. *Imperial Leather: Race, Gender, and Sexuality in the Colonial Contest*. New York: Routledge.

McConahay, John B. 1986. "Modern Racism, Ambivalence, and the Modern Racism Scale." In John F. Dovidio and Samuel L. Gaertner, eds., *Prejudice, Discrimination, and Racism*. Orlando, FL: Academic Press, pp. 91–125.

McIntosh, Peggy. 1989. "White Privilege: Unpacking the Invisible Knapsack." *Peace and Freedom Magazine*, July/August: 10–12.

Merton, Robert K. 1949. "Discrimination and the American Creed." In Robert M. MacIver, ed., *Discrimination and National Welfare*. New York: Harper and Brothers, pp. 99–126.

Merva, Mary and Richard Fowles. 2000. "Economic Outcomes and Mental Health." In Ray Marshall, ed., *Back to Shared Prosperity: The Growing Inequality of Wealth and Income in America*. Armonk, NY: M. E. Sharpe, pp. 69–75.

Miles, Robert and Malcolm Brown. 2003. *Racism*, second edition. London: Routledge.

Mishel, Lawrence. 2006. "CEO-to-Worker Pay Imbalance Grows." Economic Policy Institute. Online, available at: www.epi.org/economic_snapshots/entry/webfeatures_snapshots_20060621.

Mishel, Lawrence, Jared Bernstein, and Heather Boushey. 2003. *The State of Working America 2002/2003*. Ithaca, NY: Cornell University Press.

Modood, Tariq. 2007. *Multiculturalism*. Cambridge: Polity.

Montaigne, Michel de. 1958. *Complete Essays of Montaigne*, translated by Donald Frame. Stanford, CA: Stanford University Press.

NAACP Legal Defense Fund. 2004. *Racial Statistics of Executions and Death Row in the United States*. Formerly available online at: www.naacpldf.org/deathpenaltyinfo.

Nairn, Tom. 1977. *The Break Up of Britain*. London: New Left Books.

Nairn, Tom. 2000. *After Britain*. London: Granta.

Newman, Katherine S. 1999. *No Shame in My Game: The Working Poor in the Inner City*. New York: Vintage Books and the Russell Sage Foundation.

Newman, William. 1973. *American Pluralism: A Study of Minority Groups and Social Theory*. New York: Harper & Row.

Nicholson, Linda. 2008. *Identity before Identity Politics*. Cambridge: Cambridge University Press.

Ogbu, John. 1978. *Minority Education and Caste: The American System in Cross-Cultural Perspective*. San Diego, CA: Academic Press.

Oliver, Melvin L. and Thomas M. Shapiro. 1997. *Black Wealth/White Wealth: A New Perspective on Racial Equality*. New York: Routledge.

Olzak, Susan. 1992. *The Dynamics of Ethnic Competition and Conflict*. Stanford, CA: Stanford University Press.

Omi, Michael and Howard Winant. 1994. *Racial Formation in the United States: From the 1960s to the 1990s*. New York: Routledge.

Painter, Nell Irvin. 2010. *The History of White People*. New York: W. W. Norton.

Parekh, Bhiku. 2000. *Rethinking Multiculturalism: Cultural Diversity and Political Theory*. London: Macmillan.

Park, Robert E. 1914. "Racial Assimilation in Secondary Groups, with Particular Reference to the Negro." *American Journal of Sociology*, 19(5): 606–623.

Park, Robert E. 1950[1926]. *Race and Culture*. New York: Free Press.

Patterson, Orlando. 1997. *The Ordeal of Integration: Progress and Resentment in America's "Racial" Crisis*. Washington, DC: Civitas/Counterpoint.

Pettigrew, Thomas and Roel W. Meertens. 1995. "Subtle and Blatant Prejudice in Western Europe." *European Journal of Social Psychology*, 8(3): 241–273.

Pettigrew, Thomas and Roel W. Meertens. 2001. "In Defense of the Subtle Prejudice Concept: A Retort." *European Journal of Social Psychology*, 31(4): 299–309.

Pilkington, Andrew. 2003. *Racial Disadvantage and Ethnic Diversity in Britain*. New York: Palgrave Macmillan.

Pong, Suet-ling. 1998. "The School Compositional Effect of Single Parenthood on 10th-Grade Achievement." *Sociology of Education*, 71(1): 23–42.

Portes, Alejandro. 1998. "Social Capital: Its Origins and Applications in Modern Sociology. *Annual Review of Sociology*, 24: 1–24.

Portes, Alejandro. 2003. "Conclusion: Theoretical Convergences and Empirical Evidence in the Study of Immigrant Transnationalism." *International Migration Review*, 37(3): 874–892.

Portes, Alejandro and Rubén G. Rumbaut. 2001. *Legacies: The Story of the Second Generation Immigrant*. Berkeley, CA: University of California Press.

Portes, Alejandro and Min Zhou. 1993. "The New Second Generation: Segmented Assimilation and Its Variants." *Annals of the American Academy of Political and Social Science*, 530(November): 74–96.

Portes, Alejandro, Luis Guarnizo, and Patricia Landolt. 1999. "The Study of Transnationalism: Pitfalls and Promise of an Emergent Research Field." *Ethnic and Racial Studies*, 22(2): 217–237.

Quillian, Lincoln. 1995. "Prejudice as a Response to Perceived Group Threat: Population Composition and Anti-Immigrant and Racial Prejudice in Europe." *American Sociological Review*, 60(4): 586–611.

Quillian, Lincoln. 1996. "Group Threat and Regional Change in Attitudes toward African-Americans." *American Journal of Sociology*, 102(3): 816–860.

Rank, Mark Robert. 2004. *One Nation, Underprivileged: Why American Poverty Affects Us All*. New York: Oxford University Press.

Ripley, William Z. 1899. *The Races of Europe: A Sociological Study*. New York: D. Appleton and Company.

Roediger, David. 2005. *Working toward Whiteness: How America's Immigrants became White: The Strange Journey from Ellis Island to the Suburbs*. New York: Basic Books.

Roscigno, Vincent J. and James W. Ainsworth-Darnell. 1999. "Race, Cultural Capital and Educational Resources: Persistent Inequalities and Achievement Returns." *Sociology of Education*, 72(2): 158–178.

Said, Edward. 1979. *Orientalism*. New York: Vintage.

Sanderson, Stephen K. 2007. "Conflict Theory." In George Ritzer, ed., *The Blackwell Encyclopedia of Sociology, Vol. III*. Malden, MA: Blackwell, pp. 662–665.

Schlesinger Jr., Arthur. 1992. *The Disuniting of America: Reflections on a Multicultural Society*. New York: W. W. Norton.

Schuman, Howard, Charlotte Steeh, and Lawrence Bobo. 1997. *Racial Attitudes in America: Trends and Interpretations*, revised edition. Cambridge, MA: Harvard University Press.

Sears, David, Jim Sidanius, and Lawrence Bobo, eds. 2000. *Racialized Politics: The Debate about Racism in America*. Chicago, IL: University of Chicago Press.

Sidanius, Jim, Erik Devereux, and Felicia Pratto. 1992. "A Comparison of Symbolic Racism Theory and Social Dominance Theory as Explanations for Racial Policy Attitudes." *Journal of Social Psychology*, 132(5): 377–395.

Silberman, Roxane, Richard Alba, and Irène Fournier. 2007. "Segmented Assimilation in France? Discrimination in the Labour Market against the Second Generation." *Ethnic and Racial Studies*, 30(1): 1–27.

Smith, Anthony D. 1986. *The Ethnic Origins of Nations*. Oxford: Blackwell.

Smith, Robert C. 2006. *Mexican New York: Transnational Lives of New Immigrants*. Berkeley, CA: University of California Press.

Sniderman, Paul and Edward G. Carmines. 1997. *Reaching beyond Race*. Cambridge, MA: Harvard University Press.

Sniderman, Paul and Louk Hagendoorn. 2009. *When Ways of Life Collide: Multiculturalism and Its Discontents in the Netherlands*. Princeton, NJ: Princeton University Press.

Sniderman, Paul and Thomas L. Piazza. 1993. *The Scar of Race*. Cambridge, MA: The Belknap Press of Harvard University Press.

Sniderman, Paul and Philip E. Tetlock. 1986. "Symbolic Racism: Problems of Motive Attribution in Political Analysis." *Journal of Social Issues*, 42(2): 129–150.

Sollors, Werner. 1986. *Beyond Ethnicity: Consent and Descent in American Culture*. New York: Oxford University Press.

Steinberg, Stephen. 2007. *Race Relations: A Critique*. Stanford, CA: Stanford Social Sciences of Stanford University Press.

Straus, Scott. 2006. *The Order of Genocide: Race, Power, and War in Rwanda*. Ithaca, NY: Cornell University Press.

Street, Paul. 2005. *Segregated Schools: Educational Apartheid in Post-Civil Rights America*. New York: Routledge.

Taylor, Charles. 1992. *Multiculturalism and "The Politics of Recognition,"* with commentaries by Amy Gutmann, et al. Princeton, NJ: Princeton University Press.

Tilly, Charles. 1998. *Durable Inequality*. Berkeley, CA: University of California Press.

Trepagnier, Barbara. 2010. *Silent Racism: How Well-Meaning White People Perpetuate the Racial Divide*. Boulder, CO: Paradigm.

US Census Bureau. 2001. *Historical Income Tables: People*. Tables P-2, P-40, and P-54. Formerly available online at: www.census.gov/hhes/income/histinc/incperdet.html.

US Census Bureau. 2003. *Historical Income Tables: Households*. Table H-3. Formerly available online at: www.census.gov/hhes/income/histinc/h03.html.

US Census Bureau. 2009. *Current Population Survey*. Online, available at: www.census.gov/hhes/www/income/data/historical/inequality/index.html.

Waldinger, Roger. 2003. "Foreigners Transformed: International Migration and the Remaking of a Divided People." *Diaspora*, 12(2): 247–272.

Wallman, Sandra. 1986. "Ethnicity and the Boundary Process in Context." In John Rex and David Mason, eds., *Theories of Race and Ethnic Relations*. Cambridge: Cambridge University Press, pp. 226–245.

Warner, W. Lloyd. 1963. *Yankee City*. New Haven, CT: Yale University Press.

Warner, W. Lloyd and Leo Srole. 1945. *The Social Systems of American Ethnic Groups*. New Haven, CT: Yale University Press.

Waters, Mary. 1990. *Ethnic Options: Choosing Identities in America*. Berkeley, CA: University of California Press.

Weller, Christian E. 2010. "Economic Snapshot for December 2010." Center for American Progress. Online, available at: www.americanprogress. org/issues/2010/12/econsnap1210.html.

Wilson, William Julius. 1987. *The Truly Disadvantaged: The Inner City, the Underclass, and Public Policy*. Chicago, IL: University of Chicago Press.

Wilson, William Julius. 1996. *When Work Disappears: The World of the New Urban Poor*. New York: Alfred A. Knopf.

Wilson, William Julius. 1999. *The Bridge over the Racial Divide: Rising Inequality and Coalition Politics*. Berkeley, CA and New York: University of California Press and the Russell Sage Foundation.

Wimmer, Andreas. 2008. "The Making and Unmaking of Ethnic Boundaries: A Multilevel Process Theory." *American Journal of Sociology*, 113(4): 970–1022.

Wimmer, Andreas, Lars-Erik Cederman, and Brian Min. 2009. "Ethnic Politics and Armed Conflict: A Configurational Analysis of a New Global Data Set." *American Sociological Review*, 74(2): 316–337.

Winant, Howard. 1997. "Behind Blue Eyes: Whiteness and Contemporary US Racial Politics." *New Left Review*, 225(September/October): 73–88.

Yinger, John. 1986. "Measuring Racial Discrimination with Fair Housing Audits: Caught in the Act." *The American Economic Review*, 76(6): 881–893.

Young, Iris Marion. 1990. *Justice and the Politics of Difference*. Princeton, NJ: Princeton University Press.

INDEX

ROUTLEDGE

The Routledge Companion to Race and Ethnicity

The Routledge Companion to Race and Ethnicity

Edited by Stephen M, Caliendo and Charlton D. McIlwain,

The Routledge Companion to Race and Ethnicity is a comprehensive guide to the increasingly relevant, broad and ever changing terrain of studies surrounding race and ethnicity. Comprising a series of essays and a critical dictionary of key names and terms written by respected scholars from a range of academic disciplines, this book provides a thought provoking introduction to the field, and covers:

- The history and relationship between "race" and ethnicity
- The impact of colonialism and post colonialism
- Emerging concepts of "whiteness"
- Changing political and social implications of race
- Race and ethnicity as components of identity
- The interrelatedness and intersectionality of race and ethnicity with gender and sexual orientation
- Globalization, media, popular culture and their links with race and ethnicity

Fully cross referenced throughout, with suggestions for further reading and international examples, this book is indispensible reading for all those studying issues of race and ethnicity across the humanities and social and political sciences.

Pb: 978-0-415-77707-0
Hb: 978-0-415-77706-3

D0002433

For more information and to order a copy visit
www.routledge.com/9780415777070

Available from all good bookshops